CONCILIUM

Religion in the Eighties

CONCILIUM

Editorial Directors

Concilium 176 (6/1984): Third World Theology

CONCILIUM

List of Members

Advisory Committee: Third World Theology

Directors:

Leonardo Boff OFM	Petrópolis	Brazil
Virgil Elizondo	San Antonio, Texas	USA

Members:

K. C. Abraham	Bangalore	India
Duraisamy Amalorpavadass	Bangalore	India
Hugo Assmann	Piracicaba	Brazil
Georges Casalis	Noyon	France
F. Chikane	Pretoria	South Africa
Zwinglio Mota Dias	Rio de Janeiro	Brazil
Enrique Dussel	Mexico City	Mexico
Gustavo Gutiérrez	Lima	Peru
François Houtart	Louvain-la-Neuve	Belgium
Joâo Batista Libanio	Belo Horizonte	Brazil
Beatriz Melano Couch	Buenos Aires	Argentine
José Míguez Bonino	Buenos Aires	Argentine
Uriel Molina Oliú	Managua	Nicaragua
Ronaldo Muñoz	Santiago	Chile
John Mutiso-Mbinda	Nairobi	Kenya
Alphonse Ngindu Mushete	Kinshasa	Zaïre
M. A. Oduyoye	Ibadan	Nigeria
Soon-Kyung Park	Seoul	Korea
Juan Hernandez Pico SJ	Mexico City	Mexico
Aloysius Pieris SJ	Gonawala-Kelaniya	Sri Lanka
Samuel Rayan SJ	Delhi	India
Pablo Richard	San José	Costa Rica
J. Russel Chandran	Bangalore	India
Anselme Titanma Sanon	Upper Volta	Africa
Jon Sobrino	San Salvador	El Salvador
Sergio Torres	Santiago	Chile

THE
PEOPLE OF GOD
AMIDST
THE POOR

Edited by
Leonardo Boff
and
Virgil Elizondo

English Language Editor
Marcus Lefébure

T. & T. CLARK LTD
Edinburgh

December 1984
T. & T. Clark Ltd, 36 George Street, Edinburgh EH2 2LQ
ISBN: 0 567 30056 0

ISSN: 0010-5236

Typeset by C. R. Barber & Partners (Highlands) Ltd, Fort William
Printed in Scotland by Blackwood, Pillans & Wilson Ltd, Edinburgh

Concilium: Published February, April, June, August, October, December.
Subscriptions 1984: USA: US$40.00 (including air mail postage and packing); Canada:
Canadian$50.00 (including air mail postage and packing); UK and rest of the world:
£19.00 (including postage and packing).

CONTENTS

Part III
A Systematic Reflection on the People of God in the midst of the Poor

English Language Editor's Note

THE DIFFICULTIES of the subject discussed in this issue are substantial rather than linguistic. They have to do with the particular class structure in Latin America as compared with that in North America or Europe and the relationship between sociological and theological concepts, let alone the ecclesial implications of this new balance and tension between the political and the theological. The basic problems do, however, express themselves linguistically. They are concentrated in two terms in particular: 'people' and 'popular'. But another difficulty is that the usage does not seem to be standardised between any two authors so that one important aspect of this whole complex of problems is precisely the flux it is still in. Since the main languages from which most of the articles are translated are Spanish and Portuguese, it seemed sensible to indicate the original terms employed in brackets, at least in important instances. This seems to be the best way in which to help the evolving process of clarification to which this issue is so signal a contribution.

Editorial
The People of God among the Poor

THE SO-CALLED 'popular church' (*Igreja Popular*) has in recent years become a source of discord. To many it is a sign of hope because it shows the Church present among the poor; to others it gives cause for fear because of the risk of division in the ecclesial community. John Paul II, speaking to the Latin American bishops at Puebla on 28 January 1979, rejected the dichotomy of an 'institutional' or 'official' Church and a different 'popular church born of the people and taking shape among the poor' (Puebla 1,8). In August 1982, in a letter to the Nicaraguan bishops, he declared emphatically, 'It is absurd and dangerous to envisage, as it were alongside—not to say in opposition to—the Church structured around the bishops, another church seen as "charismatic", non-institutional, "new" and non-traditional, alternative and, as it has come to be described recently, a "popular church" ' (*Osservatore Romano*, 8 August 1982). The pope repeated these words when he spoke in Managua on 4 March 1983 before more than half a million people (cf *Osservatore Romano*, 13 April 1983).

On the other hand, the pope himself stated that the 'popular church', or 'the church born of the people' (*Igreja que nasce do povo*) can have an acceptable sense. This is the case when 'a community of people . . . open themselves to the Good News of Jesus Christ and begin to live it in a communion of faith, love, hope, prayer and celebration' (*Osservatore Romano*, 8 August 1982). In his encyclical *Laborem Exercens* the pope stated that the Church's fidelity to Christ was shown when, through its solidarity with exploited workers, it became genuinely 'the Church of the poor'(§ 8).

At the general assembly of CELAM held between 9 and 14 March 1983, stress was laid on a number of recommendations, including the following, 'CELAM should make available to episcopal conferences theological reflections on the question of the popular church, also taking into account social, economic and political aspects' (REB 1983, 412).

This issue of *Concilium*, devoted to the popular church or the church of the poor, or again the people of God among the poor, may be regarded, in a sense, as a response to this appeal. Dealing seriously with this subject requires a measure of critical distance towards the polemics which have been generated on the subject of the popular church, particularly as a result of the pope's observations.

We are pleased to note that the various contributors have succeeded in following this rule of objectivity, which is a contribution to making the Church inserted into the world of the wretched of the earth true and authentic. Whenever the cause of the poor is at issue—as in this discussion—we should proceed with care; anxiety to pull up a few weeds may lead us to uproot too much wheat and spill new wine poured into old wineskins. By so doing we would disappoint the hopes of the poor who, at least in Latin America, have found the Gospel to be a force for complete liberation, and the Church to be a space in which they can live with human dignity and as children of God. We should not provide arguments for those who insist that, historically, the Church has almost always supported the cause of the powerful by taking a paternalistic attitude towards the poor and stifling their libertarian ideals of a different society.

There can be no doubt about the situation we are currently witnessing. Many bishops, priests, men and woman religious and lay people, inspired by the Gospel and with a renewed sense of the Church's social mission, are moving more and more into poor environments; they are taking up a position of incarnation in popular culture. In this way they have enabled the Church to become the Church of ordinary people (*a Igreja se fizesse popular*). At the same time this has made it possible for the people (o povo) (the social group consisting of those with no share in power or in cultural life) to feel and regard themselves as genuinely the Church by increasingly participating in the responsibilities of the Church. It is this mutuality which is characteristic of the popular church in the true sense of the expression. It is not a matter of a division within the one Church, with the institution on one side and the faithful in their communities on the other; what we are seeing is the formation of what the National Conference of Bishops of Brazil called 'a new way of being the church' (*Comunidades Eclesiais de Base na Igreja do Brasil*, Sao Paulo 1982, n. 3). The whole Church (bishops, presbyters, laity and religious) has embarked on a process of movement from the centre to the periphery; the Church's social base is beginning to be made up more and more of the poor sectors of the population (*estratos pobres da população*). The Church is not just adopting the dominant culture (which in the Western world is under the control of the bourgeoisie), but is also inserting itself into the culture of the lower classes, giving particular characteristics to its language, celebrations, forms of organisation and theological reflection. This phenomenon is significant in Latin America; as we shall see in this issue of *Concilium*, it exists in Africa and also, in germ, in Asia.

The material of this issue is organised along three main axes: the people of God among the poor in the past and today (I), the redefinition of roles in the Church in the light of the experience of the Church of the poor (II), and a systematic reflection on the people of God among the poor (III).

The first section attempts to describe the phenomenon of the structure and functioning of a popular ecclesial community, the basis of what is called the 'popular church', in Latin America (Uriel Molina Oliú). The popular church can be seen as part of a larger process of mobilisation among the poorer classes in search of their liberation (Pablo Richard). How does a people become the people of God? An answer is offered by the exegete George Prixley in the light of the people of God in the Bible. The well-known Italian historian Giuseppe Alberigo, in a powerful synthesis, shows the vicissitudes experienced by the poor within the Church, as it oscillated between a community model which made possible a genuine and differentiated involvement by all and a society-based model which introduced the main legal division between laity and clergy. Another historian, the Latin American Enrique Dussel, studies the various meanings, and also the ambiguities, associated with the expression 'people of God' in the recent documents of Vatican II (1965), Medellín (1968) and Puebla (1979).

In the second part reflection gives way to testimony. How are the various ecclesial functions being redefined and how are new ministries emerging? Cardinal Aloisio Lorscheider describes his own process of 'conversion' as a result of a fraternal sharing of the lives of the people and the poor. John Mutiso-Mbinda describes how the specifically priestly identity of his own ministry was enriched among the poor. His religious life was strengthened in his experience of God and his sense of mission through being rooted in the situation of the poor. The well-known theologian of liberation Gustavo Gutiérrez traces his own theological development from the challenges presented by the oppressed, marginalised groups and subject races. Three lay coordinators (Carlos Zarco Mera, Carlos Manuel Sánchez and Leonor Tellería) describe their service in their basic ecclesial communities. Finally Casiano Floristán shows how all pastoral practices conceal a model of the Church being constructed consciously or unconsciously. In the popular church, which is made up of a vast network of communities, the model can be seen as communitarian, prophetic, liberating and missionary.

The last section attempts to analyse the terms of the discussion. What elements go to make up the meaning of 'people' (*povo*)? Few words are as ideologically charged as this.

Pedro Ribeiro de Oliveira has made a notable attempt to construct the category analytically in such a way as to make it an intellectual tool which enables us to understand better the reality of the popular church. Leonardo Boff has tried, in close connection with the conclusions of Pedro Ribeiro de Oliveira, to cleanse the concept of 'people of God' of its inadequate uses, which encourage either a spiritualisation of the reality of the Church as a historical instrument of salvation or ecclesiastical populism. The popular church, as it is developing in Latin America, is one historical embodiment (among a number of possible forms) of the theological concept of the people of God. Lastly Professor Edward Schillebeeckx studies the new distribution of sacral power in the community-communion model of the Church, a distribution which makes possible greater participation on the part of all.

We hope that these studies will help Christians to understand better what the popular church represents: the effort of significant sections of the Church to enter the world of the poor and create possibilities for the poor to become, in reality, the Church. Only in this way does 'the church of the poor' become a reality rather than a piece of rhetoric.

VIRGIL ELIZONDO
LEONARDO BOFF

Translated by Francis McDonagh

PART I

The People of God amidst the Poor Yesterday and Today

Uriel Molina Oliú

How a People's Christian Community (*Comunidad Cristiana Popular*) is Structured and how it Functions

1. ITS ORIGIN

UNTIL 1961, Managua, with a population of about 200,000, had only two parishes. A better parochial arrangement was necessary, if the pastoral needs of the outlying districts of Managua were to be met. At that time, El Riguero had 20,000 inhabitants. Pastoral care in this deprived area was limited to an occasional visit from a priest to say mass or to celebrate Holy Week. A few nuns were responsible for preparing children for their first communion.

In October 1965—after twelve years of studying philosophy and theology in Italy, Germany and Jerusalem—I became involved in the pastoral work of the parish of Our Lady of Fátima in the El Riguero district of Managua. This was a parish which had been under the pastoral care of Italian Franciscan Fathers from Assisi, and was part of the new parochial arrangement in the capital city of Managua. The Franciscans had built the church, the religious house and a dispensary. Their pastoral activity had been in the traditional mould. I decided, therefore, to start work along the lines suggested by the Second Vatican Council, which had just come to an end. I began to invite the faithful to meet me, so that I could explain to them what was needed in these modern days, and these meetings gradually developed into a regular Bible School, which went on for about ten years.

My first sessions on the Bible were limited to providing introductory material and replying to criticisms. A little later we worked through a course on the History of Salvation. The task was not an easy one. Those simple people, weary from their day's work, illiterate, and accustomed only to a folk-lore type of Catholicism, were not able properly to tackle Bible-study. But they were very willing, and with the help of biblical maps and colour-slides they learnt about the land where Jesus lived, and so acquired a real desire to get to know the Bible.

The Conference at Medellín (1968) helped the communities in Nicaragua to understand the Council from the standpoint of their own actual experience. It happened in this way:

the Second Vatican Council came to an end officially in 1965, a year after the foundation of the Frente Sandinista de Liberación Nacional. From then on there were two parallel renewal movements in Nicaragua. On one side there was the Frente Sandinista, the early stages of a movement for liberation by means of an armed struggle; and on the other side, within the Church, there was a timid impulse towards renewal along the lines suggested by the Council. The Frente Sandinista represents a genuine new social and political force in Nicaragua, over against the traditional political parties. It set out to follow the example of Sandino and recover the national identity which had so often been compromised through North American interference, with the approval of the oligarchical political parties. Both movements developed independently until Medellín was able to bridge the gap and bring them together. Christians began to find renewal as they organised themselves into basic communities. Examples of such communities are: the Community of St. Paul the Apostle, set up in the 14th September district, which modelled itself increasingly on the Community of Little Saint Michael in Panama, and which produced the Nicaraguan Mass; Ernesto Cardenal's Community of Solentiname, from which there emerged a new interpretation of the Psalms and of the Gospel; and the rural communities of the Pacific, which were supported and helped by Father Gaspar García Laviana, together with a team of priests and lay-people. There were also movements among students at secondary and university level. These displayed a growing desire to combine the claims of Christianity with the revolutionary struggle.

In El Riguero, various basic Christian communities were very quickly formed. The main characteristic of these communities was that, over a period of two years, they had in their fellowship a group of university students who were trying to live out their faith among poor and simple people. One of the students put it in this way: '. . . There we realised that we had to have a more direct relationship with ordinary people. And, on the other hand, there was at that point a wearing away of what had been our religious experience. It became very firmly established that we had to see faith not as an individual, but as a collective, affair. We had to try to communicate with the people, to be alongside the oppressed, to engage in the struggle for justice. All these questions seemed to us to have no place in the familiar, university environment in which we normally moved. This led us, or at least led me, to two conclusions: first, that faith could not be lived in an individual way, but had to be lived collectively; and secondly that faith could not be authentic if it was not related to the poor and the exploited. Probably at that moment we had no conception of a class-structure in Nicaraguan society, but we were certainly aware, in general terms, of the poor. Then, on the strength of these two basic ideas, we began to concern ourselves with the idea of creating a life-community, a work-community.' These Christians, in their community-groups, made a very significant contribution to the struggle of the Frente Sandinista, because they made possible a broadening of the social base of the Sandinista movement. In fact, the Frente was suffering some very hard blows in the mountain areas, and was finding it necessary to move its struggle from the countryside to the city. Thus there arose the necessity for contact between Christians and revolutionaries. The ground was, as it were, already prepared, and so Christians joined in the struggle from within the Frente. They went underground, and were prepared to compromise themselves in the struggle for liberation.

2. DESCRIPTION OF THE BASIC CHRISTIAN COMMUNITY

The basic community was in no way similar to such traditional apostolic movements as the Legion of Mary, the Marian Congregation, the Apostolate of Prayer, etc. Nor had it anything to do with the 'Short Courses in Christianity' movements (Cursillos). The latter arose in the upper and middle classes. They did not establish clearly the link between faith and politics. Nevertheless they became very widespread, and many of those who belonged to them later joined the Frente and shared in the popular rising.

In the basic communities, the members were poor, sometimes unemployed, sometimes underemployed. Their consciousness was quickly aroused by the method proposed at Medellín: 'See, judge and act.' One day, for example, it happened that milk had suddenly gone up considerably in price. This situation, which affected the poor, was made the subject of reflection by the community. The university people, following their methods of socio-political analysis, came to the conclusion that this injustice could only be overcome as the poor were made aware of their condition and became organised. Then came the moment of biblical enlightenment. We took 1 Timothy 6:6–10 and 17–19: 'Religion, of course, does bring large profits, but only to those who are content with what they have. We brought nothing into the world, and we can take nothing out of it; but as long as we have food and clothing, let us be content with that. . . . The love of money is the root of all evils. . . . Warn those who are rich in this world's goods that they are . . . not to set their hopes on money, which is untrustworthy, but on God, who, out of his riches, gives us all that we need for our happiness. Tell them . . . to be generous and willing to share.'

We had to relate our biblical insights to the actual situation. The Bible provided us with the basic impulse, which pushed us into the struggle for the transformation of the existing state of affairs. In order to achieve it, we needed socio-political means. For example, the Bible tells us, in the passage quoted: 'let us be content with our food and clothing'. Our reflection led us to the concept of a new society, where people's primary needs would be satisfied (education for all, food for all, housing for all, health for all). The Bible also says: 'tell the rich to be willing to share their goods.' Social analysis led us to recognise that society is badly organised, and organised for the benefit of privileged minorities. The rich needed to be persuaded to change. The conclusion we came to was that they would never do it willingly, and that therefore, if the message was to be effective, it would be necessary to pass through a structural revolution. The meeting finally decided on a concrete symbolic gesture: we would scatter nails along the streets where the milk-lorries would pass, and puncture their tyres. The drivers of the vehicles would then be persuaded to allow the young people to distribute the milk to the children. In this way the community meeting was not simply a time of reflection and analysis, but also of organisation for the struggle.

(a) Bible and community life

Anyone who has practical experience of a basic community recognises immediately that the poor have a sort of sixth sense which enables them to grasp the message of the Bible. The poor know that the Bible speaks for them, so that, when they read a passage carefully, they immediately begin to give very colourful and eloquent expression to it. An example of this is to be found in Ernesto Cardenal's book: *El Evangelio en Solentiname*. We in El Riguero did not write down our experience. Our fundamental starting-point was the Exodus. In this way the community learnt how to discover a God who was not the God of the catechism, a God of good order, but the God of the poor, one who listens to the cry of the oppressed. The young people were very fond of Daniel 3, where three young men refuse to worship the statue of Nebuchadnezzar. Thus they learnt from their faith not to yield, but to continue the struggle.

We spent many hours in trying to understand the true meaning of Christian conversion (*metanoia*). The people had been so strongly influenced by a pietistic kind of Catholicism that I found it hard to get them to understand conversion as a change of mind and attitude towards the offer of the Gospel. In my community, the biblical passages which proved most basic for the building up of the community were: the Exodus; the prophets, especially Isaiah 58, Micah, Amos, Deutero-Isaiah and Daniel 3; and, in the New Testament, Luke 4, the Beatitudes, Matthew 25, 1 Corinthians, James, and, in general, all passages concerning the New Man.

(b) Prayer and community

Prayer was always an extremely important element in the life of the community. We almost always prayed in a communal way. Prayer came to be the sharing of a social need, which was then offered to the Lord. We held spiritual retreats for leaders, but the ordinary people expressed themselves best in the great festivals of the liturgical year. In the Holy Week celebrations, it was a matter of expressing, through the Passion of Christ, the pain of a suffering people. The wooden cross carried by the Nazarene was covered with newspaper cuttings containing reports of deaths and disappearances, or protests about the violation of human rights. The young men preached the Via Crucis in the streets, as they denounced the atrocities committed under the dictatorship of Somoza. The vigil of Holy Saturday was also very well attended. There were no public readings, but rather study-groups around bonfires. In these, the meditation centred on three points: the Hebrew Passover, the Passover of Jesus, and the Passover of our people (*nuestro pueblo*). We were greatly helped by no. 5 in the Introduction to the Medellín statement: 'We cannot fail to hear the step of the Lord who saves us, when we pass from less human conditions to more human ones...' The ceremony ended with a procession led by a cross of flowers, symbolising the resurrection and the hope of our people.

Often there were vigils, particularly to protest against the dictatorship. We learnt to live out our faith in conflict. And numbers grew every day of those who wanted to join the community and, because of their faith, commit themselves to the popular movement (*movimiento popular*).

(c) Mobilisation of the people in the light of the Bible

Basic Christian communities have certainly played a leading role in the renewal of the Church. In the First Pastoral Care Week (January 1969) they were regarded as the best possible means of evangelisation and pastoral care. Between 1969 and 1972 a vast movement was developing in the Church which was to have led to a Consultation on Pastoral Care at national level. It was a period of great richness, and brought about a deepening of faith, a greater political involvement on the part of Christians, the emergence of new forms of ministry, and the closer unity of Christians over the question of the liberation of the poor. This was the only time that all of us in Nicaragua—people, priests, religious and bishops—have found ourselves united in the running of the Church. Regrettably the planned Consultation on Pastoral Care could not take place at national level, because in September 1972 the Social Secretariat of CELAM sent out a letter advising against it, since, according to them, it would have come under the control of Marxist elements. Some months later the devastating earthquake occurred. Thus pastoral organisation fell apart, and neocatechumenal and charismatic movements found their way into the Church, bringing a totally different approach.

The community of El Riguero played a very important part during the period of agitation between 1974 and 1977. Christian people felt the need to become organised and perform acts of solidarity with, and support for, the Frente Sandinista. The commonest forms of mobilisation of the people consisted in the taking over of churches to denounce injustices and rally popular support, and in processions organised from the church steps. On one occasion, the community met as usual on the steps of the church. The parish cook, an old woman called Julia, took the Bible, opened it at the second book of Maccabees, and began to read chapter 7, which relates the famous exhortation of a Hebrew mother to her seven sons, telling them to suffer martyrdom rather than betray the faith of their fathers. The reading turned into a veritable harangue, interspersed with slogans and chants: 'People, unite!' So began the procession through the streets of the district. Many of these processions ended in violence, with tear-gas, salvos of grape-shot, and blows from sticks or rifle-butts. This is what happened when Somaza banned news bulletins over the radio. Many priests lent their church microphones to the journalists, and the people came together in crowds to hear what was happening in the country. This kind of gathering is known in Nicaragua as 'catacomb journalism'. Often the meeting would begin and end with a hymn and biblical meditation. The bishops condemned the journalists as profaners. But among the people the conviction steadily grew that at that particular time the Church had a role of prophetic denunciation to fulfil.

(d) Hierarchy and parish community

The community felt increasingly that it was the Church of Christ in El Riguero. Many times it expressed its pastoral feeling to the bishop, sending him letters which showed how very conscious it was of belonging to the Church. Regrettably the bishop never entered into dialogue with the community, except indirectly, through his chaplain. However, a more mature church was coming into being. New forms of ministry were developing, and a basic ecumenism was taking shape.

(e) Difficulties in the way of involvement in the political struggle

The main difficulty was always that of accepting armed violence as the way of liberation. The atrocities committed by Somoza were, however, leading gradually to the conviction that, while it may be true that violence is not part of the Gospel, nevertheless, as Paul VI teaches in *Populorum Progressio*, one must not 'abuse a people's patience'. Another difficulty was that of reconciling Christian love with the class-struggle. We came to the conclusion that we can and must love our enemy even while we are fighting him to bring about his conversion. It was also difficult to reconcile risk with the practice of the faith. We Christians were not accustomed, like the Sandinistas, to run risks for our cause. We had also to learn how to rid ourselves of a purist conception of life, and how to get our hands dirty. At the same time we had to free ourselves from the constant suspicion that perhaps we were just tools of the Sandinistas.

(f) Testimonies of faith in the community

Every Christian felt it was his duty to put himself at risk by giving shelter to the freedom-fighters. Amid the suffering, all kinds of testimonies began to appear. The old women and children of the community served as messengers to the safe houses where the guerrillas were accommodated. Sometimes the guerrillas would emerge from their hiding-places—as one did on the day Doña Julia died, to offer the old woman a love-poem, in honour of her womb, as mother of the New Man: 'Venerable womb, unfaltering. . . .' When they tortured David, he wrote me many letters: 'My brother: I don't know whether it's day or night. I am naked. A guard stood over me and wounded my testicles. I am passing blood. Tell the community that I am offering all my sufferings to the Lord, for the sake of the New Humanity we want to build.' I replied with phrases from biblical texts strung together, and sent him the eucharist so that in prison he might share communion with his companions. Never was the prayer-life of the community so intense as during the imprisonment of David. His sufferings confirmed the faith of many—including my own. . . . His words gave me courage at those times when it seemed that we had lost all hope.

Today stories of selfless devotion come in one after the other. A little while ago, a mother asked me to say a mass for her son who had died in combat. Seeing her weeping, I said: 'Losing him has caused you much grief, hasn't it?' 'Yes, father', she answered, 'but the cause for which he died was greater than my womb.' All this helps us to understand the extent of the love felt for the people's cause (*la causa del pueblo*). So it was when a rocket destroyed the body of Lupita Montiel's son. Risking the heavy bombardment, Lupita collected her son's remains to give them Christian burial. They asked me to perform the funeral ceremony. The mother bent over her lifeless son in a posture of grief. I could not bring myself to uncover the body, but she invited me to do so, saying in a loud voice: 'I am proud to have borne a Sandinista son.'

3. OPENING THE DOORS TO THE SPIRIT

I think that the Sandinista revolution presented the Nicaraguan Church, and in particular the basic Christian communities, with some great challenges. It seems to me simplistic to want to leave the Christians in these communities in isolation from the institution of the Church. We Christians do not want to separate ourselves from the hierarchy. Our only desire is that there should be dialogue, and that our pastoral choice in the revolutionary situation, made in faith, should be recognised as legitimate. We have to preach the Gospel from within the developing situation, and if we are to do that we cannot go on being Christians in just the same way as we were in former times. The hierarchy must open itself up to a dialogue which will help it to reformulate the very truths of the faith in terms which can be understood by the revolutionaries, and, above all, to express the faith by acts of love and goodness. This people which has suffered so much through exploitation, through the earthquake, and through the war of liberation, is as much in need of a Good Samaritan as was the wounded man by the roadside. New signs of Christ's presence have to be set up in the midst of people mobilised for war, or picking coffee or cotton. We must also celebrate the faith in ways which take up the life and the suffering of our people, and, especially, we must not wound them by refusing mass for their heroes and martyrs. To celebrate the memory of a hero or martyr is the same as celebrating the revelation of God in his act of liberation, because we could not remember heroes if there had not been a revolution. The commemoration of a hero is the evocation of the liberating act of God in revolution. It is the celebration of the cause of an entire people.

Thus the priest is trying out a new way of being a priest. He feels himself to be a priest because at every moment he finds himself deeply involved in the death of a people which wants to defend its life. In the same way, religious dedication can be seen as a loving surrender to the cause of a people struggling to be free.

The challenges presented to the Nicaraguan Church by this revolution are so numerous and of such a kind that we shall never be able to respond to them from rigid positions. Much flexibility is needed. We need to open our doors to the Spirit, who is blowing everywhere, but has not yet succeeded in finding a chink in the houses of the bishops, so that we may acquire a better understanding of the message which the image of the breath of God wants to convey to us—the clearest message in the whole of the Bible. 'The wind blows wherever it pleases; you hear its sound, but you cannot tell where it comes from or where it is going. That is how it is with all who are born of the Spirit' (John 3:8).

There is need of much understanding, much theological reflection, much freedom of spirit to understand the signs of the times, and, above all, much humility and love, so as not to condemn what is pejoratively called 'The People's Church' (*Iglesia Popular*), but is in fact the innovatory sign of a new way of being the Church. It wants to establish itself as a right among those who see revolutionary involvement as a response to faith's demand that we should show a bias towards the poor.

Translated by G.W.S. Knowles

Pablo Richard

The Church of the Poor within the Popular Movement (*Movimiento Popular*)

THE AIM of this essay is to identify and to define the Church of the Poor within the popular movement in South America. My own experience and reflections refer principally to the last six years in Central America, especially in Nicaragua. What I mean by 'popular movement' is simply all the organisations, activities and other expressions by which the poor and the oppressed manifest their struggle for liberation and which demonstrate that the people are on the move. The term 'Church of the Poor' is synonymous with 'Church of the People', 'The Church that comes into being from the People', 'The Church amongst the People' . . . etc. It is not a question of a new Church, a parallel, clandestine or rebel Church, or an anti-Church which is in opposition to the official Church or to the hierarchy. It is simply a matter of a movement of ecclesial renewal with the Church as it exists here and now and which has come into being from the response of faith which certain sectors of the people have given to God's liberating activity in history (see *Puebla* No. 263 and *Laborem Exercens* No. 8).

1. THE IDENTIFICATION OF THE CHURCH OF THE POOR WITHIN THE POPULAR MOVEMENT

(a) The locus and forms of self expression of the Church of the Poor

The Church of the Poor does not simply consist of the sum total of all Basic Ecclesial Communities but includes all the liberating influence of these Basic Ecclesial Communities within the very nucleus of the people. These Basic Ecclesial Communities, those who work in the pastoral field and certain other ecclesial institutions are—to employ the common metaphor—only the tip of the iceberg; the invisible mass of the Church of the Poor is hidden in the depths of that sea which consists of the popular movement and religious consciousness. The impact of liberating Christian witness surpasses traditional ecclesial dimensions and creates new areas of growth for the Church of the Poor within the popular movement. It is impossible to 'measure' the presence of the Church of the Poor within the popular movement with purely quantitative criteria since these properly belong to a systematised form of Christianity.

The Church of the Poor finds its forms of self expression and its identity in a variety of ways and at differing levels within the popular movement.

(i) *Militant Christians*. As individuals, they join the movements for liberation or the people's parties. These Christians form an expression of the faith of the people to the extent that they live their faith explicitly and publicly by giving it some form of ecclesial point of reference and basing it on some theological reflection. Many of them have given their lives as martyrs for the faith. They constitute prophetic minorities recreating and interpreting the conferences of Puebla and Medellín in terms of the evangelical radicalism of Liberation Theology. They are few in number, but their witness has had a profound and effective liberating influence on the consciousness of the people at large.

(ii) *Those involved in pastoral activity*. This group comprises priests, religious and lay people with pastoral responsibilities in the Church. After a long period of pastoral activity, some of these agents become directly involved in the political organisations of the people when the very people amongst whom they have exercised a pastoral role mobilise themselves and begin to get organised for their own liberation. But the majority of these pastoral activists remain in their parishes or communities and through their work continue to help the people pastorally on their way towards political maturity. With its specific ecclesial identity, pastoral work itself becomes yet another dimension of the popular movement and in this form of pastoral work the people find a spiritual strength which allows them to take part in the revolutionary process with more awareness, autonomy and self identity.

(iii) *The Basic Ecclesial Communities*. Just as militant Christians join the liberation movements as individuals, so do the Basic Ecclesial Communities; they do so as communities, maintaining their specific ecclesial identity. The Basic Ecclesial Communities markedly contribute to the effectiveness of the work of those involved in pastoral activities and help to establish firmly that work within the consciousness of the people. The Basic Ecclesial Communities participate in the liberation movements and, within these, create a dimension within which Christians can pray, celebrate their faith and read the Bible. Thus, Basic Ecclesial Communities become a focus for liberating evangelisation and for teaching the faith to the people within the very core of the popular movement.

(iv) *The Poor and Believing People*. It is not just militant Christians, pastoral activists or the Basic Ecclesial Communities which give expression or identity to the Church of the Poor within the popular movement; the people (*pueblo*) itself, as the subject of its own history, is also capable of transforming its own *religious* consciousness. This does not happen spontaneously, neither does it happen through the direct influence of popular parties or organisations; but it occurs only because the Church of the Poor acts as a mediator and a point of reference within the popular movement. The relationship between any revolutionary process and religious consciousness is both fruitful and positive when there exists amongst the people the point of reference of a revolutionary Christianity. The people is capable of transforming an alienated religion into another liberating religion or Christian expression. The poor and believing people also emerge in the Church as a subject of ecclesial creativity. At this level, the various forms and strata of identification of the Church of the Poor within the popular movement find their best expression and true depths and render irrelevant the traditional and theoretical standards by which the presence and the strength of the Church have been gauged.

(b) The Church of the Poor and new understanding of the popular movement

The growth of the Church of the Poor within the popular movement is at one and the same time both an effect and a cause of a new political understanding of people and of popular movement. Without this new understanding, the Church of the Poor will find serious obstacles in the way of its penetration into the consciousness of the people. It is equally true that where there is no Church of the Poor, there is no development of new social and political forms of popular movement. In South America, no genuine revolution is possible without the participation of the *majorities*. Only the people, acting as a majority, with self-awareness and organised as a historical subject, can overcome the tremendous obstacles, both internal and external, which stand in the way of the popular revolution and the building up of a new society. In order that this kind of mobilisation of the people can take place, it is essential that the people see the possible attainment of two fundamental things through the revolution. On the one hand, the *basic needs* of the people must be provided, viz.; work, food, health, housing, education. . . . On the other hand, the people must attain its identity as a people. The theoretical and practical consideration of this *identity* of a people is the most basic of all the new revolutionary processes, especially in Central America where this identity plays a decisive role in the *becoming aware* of the people and in their *will* to go on until victory is won. And the religious and Christian dimension forms a constitutive element of this popular identity. The people mobilises itself when it sees the possibility of achieving its Christian identity both in the political struggle for power and in the building up of a new society. These two elements are important because the people will not accept that all concern should be about the seizure of power without it being made quite explicit from the very beginning what is intended to be achieved with the new power of the people. The Basic Ecclesial Communities have been quite aware of this experience within the community at large from the very beginning of the struggle and the attempt to build up a new society (at times paying no attention to the political implications of seizing power). When the people feel or realise that the revolution is becoming a threat to its Christian identity—whether this occurs before or after the seizure of power—then they will no longer take part in the revolution or will participate only as a minority even when the revolution objectively achieves the class interests and basic requirements of the people.

Other constitutive elements of the identity of a people include the ethnic aspect—both of Indians and Afro-Americans—and the national aspect—the geo-political and historical roots of the actual people under review. To some extent, women and youth also form constitutive parts of the identity of a people. A new political concept of people and of popular movement has to correspond not just to class interests (and the provision of basic needs) but also to the identity of a people in *all* its forms and constitutive elements. This is what is called 'the logic of majorities' in Nicaragua. Undoubtedly, the identity of a people undergoes a critical internal transformation in the revolutionary process but the continuity of that basic identity is never interrupted. This fundamental identity is what makes it possible for the people to be the subject of a revolution and to be the subject of its own internal transformation as a people as well, submitting to a positive critique all the constitutive elements of its own religious, ethnic, national and social identity. This new political understanding of a popular movement contradicts the practice and the theory of the traditional left-wing parties of South America. These have never given sufficient consideration to the identity of a people since their social composition and thinking were normally secularised, ethnically they tended to be White-orientated and they were socially chauvinistic and these features prevented them from understanding the Christian, ethnic and national reality of the people as such, far less the reality of women. This 'logic of the minorities' never created a mobilisation *en masse* of the people but it is something that is being superseded in Central America.

2. THE IDENTITY AND MISSION OF THE CHURCH OF THE POOR WITHIN THE POPULAR MOVEMENT

The theological definition of the Church of the Poor within the popular movement does not restrict the universal character of the Church. The universality of the Church of the Poor lies in its roots and in its vocation. In the very nucleus of the movement of the poor and the oppressed, the Church of the Poor searches out the presence of the living God and this is its fundamental theological root. From this presence, the Church of the Poor calls all men together for salvation; and even the oppressors of the people can recover their human and Christian condition through a process of conversion and integration into the Church of the Poor. Accordingly, the Church of the Poor does not try to account for the Church as a whole, but to be its fundamental source of conversion and renewal; neither is the Church of the Poor a sect, but is the fundamental dimension of the universal vocation of the whole Church. I shall now go on to give specific definition to this identity and mission of the Church of the Poor within the popular movement according to the classical scheme of the three constitutive dimensions of the Church—prophetic, sacramental and pastoral.

(a) Prophetic identity and mission of the Church of the Poor

The Church of the Poor puts its prophetic dimension into effect by evangelisation and by teaching the faith within the heart of the popular movement. *Evangelisation* has as its centre and object the discovery and proclamation of the true God; the God revealed in Exodus, in the Prophets, in the Gospels and in the Book of Revelation; the God of Jesus Christ who is the God of the Poor. This evangelisation is not fundamentally opposed to atheism but to idolatry and the problem is not one of trying to demonstrate the existence of God but of showing that God is with the poor in their struggle for liberation. To effect any evangelisation, the Church of the Poor must, on the one hand, stand up against the idolatrous roots of oppression and expose the falsehood of the 'transcendental' and 'supernatural' dimensions of the systems of domination. On the other hand, on discovering the God of the Poor within the liberation movement, evangelisation creates therein a dimension, a power, a spiritual force, a sense of freedom, transcendence and idealism which constitute what *Puebla* (No. 1147) calls 'the evangelising potential of the Poor'.

The Basic Ecclesial Communities have developed a practical *methodology of evangelisation* which consists of three phases; beginning as *spirituality*, it continues as *biblical discernment* and concludes as *theological reflection*. These do not represent three successive and chronological stages, but rather three logical moments which demonstrate the rationality of evangelisation or the proper and real course that evangelisation follows in our Communities. Let us look at each of these in turn.

(i) *Spirituality*. The root or the original and originating experience of all evangelisation is the experience of God in the history of the oppressed. The poor evangelise the rest of us when, in their struggles for liberation, they communicate to us their own experience of God and the 'secrets of the Kingdom' which have been revealed only to them (see Matthew 11:25). Evangelisation, therefore, is not a long and complex form of preaching *about* God but rather the sustained practice of silence which allows to develop within us the habit of listening, seeing and touching this presence of God in the history of the liberation of the oppressed. This spirituality does not become reduced to a form of individual perception but finds corporate and communal expression in many signs, celebrations, songs and prayers in which the people celebrate their faith and proclaim the God in whom they believe. One expression of that particular faith which is of special importance in Central America is the people's commemoration of their martyrs. Here, we have the most profound and dramatic corporate expression of the transcendent and spiritual dimension of the struggles for liberation. In this celebration, not only is the past remembered, but expression is also given to the absolute sense of God in the practice of that justice for which the martyr gave his life. As the first stage of evangelisation, a *sine qua non* of this kind of spirituality is a knowledge of the historical reality which emerges from a militant activism within the popular movement. This knowledge is a political necessity shared by all those who struggle for justice, but, adopted as part of the process of evangelisation, it acquires a spiritual dimension over and above its political dimension. The history of the poor provides the locus for encountering God and the one who fails to find that place can neither discover nor proclaim the God of the poor. A knowledge of reality does not take us mechanically and necessarily towards the experience of God but it is an essential condition which will render it possible for us to accept the gift and the grace of such experience. It is for this reason that the practice of evangelisation within our communities always begins with a political commitment and with an analysis of reality as necessary conditions of that spirituality which prepares us to accept the revelation of God in history. Ignorance of reality, for political or ideological reasons, not only distances us from the world of the oppressed but also incapacitates us spiritually for being able to preach the God of Jesus Christ.

(ii) *Biblical discernment.* If evangelisation begins as a spiritual experience within the movement for the liberation of the oppressed, it is essential for that evangelisation to exist that such an experience be acknowledged and shared with others. It is necessary to go from practising the faith to bearing witness to the faith and this is what allows the faith to be communicated and spread within the popular movement. This communication of the faith is normally achieved through *biblical re-reading.* The text of the Bible is not used in the communities as a direct revelation of God, but as an instrument for discerning the revelation of the living Word of God in our contemporary situation. We communicate this discernment of God in history through biblical re-reading. It is not simply a form of biblical commentary but an experience of God in the history of the oppressed which is *discerned* according to the criteria of *Bible reading* and *communicated* through *biblical re-reading.*

(iii) *Theological reflection.* All the foregoing must conclude with a theoretical confrontation with the total rationality of the practice of liberation. As a part of and an extension to a process of evangelisation effected by the Basic Ecclesial Communities within the popular movement, this theology is what allows us to give 'a reason (logos) for our hope' (1 Peter 3:15). This theology, lived within the practice of liberation, allows evangelisation to penetrate to the depths of the consciousness of the people. The Church of the Poor lives its faith in that rationality which the poor make their own, understand and make known in their struggles for liberation. By its theology, the Church of the Poor thus re-affirms its identity and prophetic mission within the popular movement.

(b) Sacramental identity and mission of the Church of the Poor

The Church of the Poor is fundamentally a 'charismatic movement' within the popular movement; today, the Church of the Poor carries on the practice and activity of Jesus amongst the poor and the oppressed; as such, the Church of the Poor possesses many of the radical, evangelical, utopian and apocalyptic characteristics of the primitive Christian communities. However, the Church of the Poor does not exclude an ecclesial institutionalisation of the faith. Its institutional strategy is not to *break off* from the institutional Church as it actually exists but *to renew* that institutionalisation radically.

The fundamental point of reference for institutional renovation for the Church of the Poor is not the preservation of the Kingdom and the Power of the Church, it is rather the affirmation of the Kingdom and the Power of God which comes to the surface within the movement of the poor and the oppressed. The Church of the Poor tries to be a sign or sacrament of the Kingdom of God in the very heart of the popular movement and in order to do so it seeks to renew the institutional Church. The Church of the Poor thus tries to put into effect institutionally the priestly or sacramental character of the people as the people of God. It is the Kingdom of God emerging in history, which discerns and continually judges every ecclesial institutionalisation of the activity of Jesus Christ throughout that history. This also demands an internal conversion of the Church; the change from internal structures of power and domination to ones of brotherly service (see Mark 10:41–45).

(c) Pastoral identity and mission of the Church of the Poor

Here, I would like to present an outline of the minimal pastoral delineation of the *pastoral profile* or *pastoral planning* of the Church of the Poor within the popular movement.

(i) The Church of the Poor must concentrate its pastoral work precisely where its greatest strength lies—within the exploited and believing people. The true strength of the Church of the Poor lies in its roots—the evangelising potential of the poor who discover and announce the liberating action of God (the Kingdom of God) in the struggles of the people for liberation. Therefore the main pastoral challenge for the Church of the Poor is precisely that of effecting 'pastoral action amongst the people'; a pastoral activity which will adopt the 'logic of the majorities' which will build up the Church as the People of God by way of pastorally leading the people of the poor and the oppressed *en masse*. The objective of this pastoral action is not to dominate but to serve the people with a pastoral action of liberation of the people's consciousness through the proclamation of the Gospel. It is necessary to build up Basic Ecclesial Communities in all the 'corners' and 'hidden places' amongst the people, not so as to organise them as 'the people of the Church' but so as to liberate them spiritually as the 'People of God'. The Church has to place itself at the service of the people and not to organise the people for serving the Church. This form of pastoral action amongst the people has to be thought out and properly structured both from 'inside out' and 'from top to bottom'. One important element in all this will be the creation of new ministries to which the poor, Indians, Blacks, youth, women, etc. will have direct access.

(ii) The Church of the Poor is not a political project and must itself never use political power to help its growth. Christians and the Basic Ecclesial Communities must live their faith within the popular movement and this implies living the faith within a process of building up the power of the people (in this sense there can be no 'apoliticking' in the Church of the Poor), but that does not mean that the Church of the Poor can use that power for itself as a Church; even less may it use that power in order to resolve the conflicts and the internal contradictions of the Church itself. The *political* power of the people could politically oppose all manipulation of the Church by the enemies of the people, but the Church of the Poor as a Church must seek support only in the power of the Gospel and the power of its own faith, hope and love. That was the 'pastoral' strategy of Jesus Christ and it brought him to the Cross but also to the Resurrection. This rejection of the use of political power by the Church of the Poor for its pastoral planning is a weakness, but in that weakness really lies its strength: the strength of the Gospel which grows from the evangelising potential of the poor.

(iii) If indeed the Church of the Poor has to grow from the faith of the people in whom she has her main source of strength and must not use the political power of the people in favour of her own pastoral plans as the Church of the Poor, it is also quite certain that the pastoral plan of the Church of the Poor must 'follow the rhythm' of historical processes. In situations of extreme oppression, the Church of the Poor normally lays special emphasis on its basic pastoral work and, to a certain extent, takes to itself the political dynamism of the people within its communities. The pastoral plan of the Church of the Poor in revolutionary contexts or in situations where revolution has been successful is quite different. In these cases, the Church of the Poor has to reach out to the whole people by creating efficient and general signs of an evangelical revolutionary Christianity. Similarly, the Basic Ecclesial Communities must effect a different dynamism: they can eventually diminish but be more effective in expressing the evangelical and spiritual dynamism which comes up out of the revolutionary process itself. In situations of oppression, the Church of the Poor is the 'voice of those who have no voice', but in revolutionary situations, the mission of the Church of the Poor is simply to give a name and ecclesial expression to that God hidden in the heart of the popular movements and in their spiritual powers for liberation.

(iv) The final element of the pastoral plan of the Church of the Poor, which I just wish to mention, is ecumenism. Nothing causes more damage to the identity and mission of the Church of the Poor than religious sectarianism and proselytism. Ecumenism affirms that the people are not the private property of any church, but that the people properly belong to God. Ecumenism demands that the churches place themselves at the service of the people as the People of God. The scandal is not just that we are divided as Christians but that we quarrel with one another from a multiplicity of religious traditions and Christian confessions instead of serving the one People of God. Ecumenism demands that we convert to the people and from the people to God.

Translated by John Angus Macdonald

Jorge Pixley

The People of God In Biblical Tradition

'People of God' (*Pueblo de Dios*) is at one and the same time a doctrine, with many variants in biblical literature, and a reference to a historical reality, which also has its variants in the course of the period of over a thousand years during which the books of the Bible were taking shape. Because of this complexity there are various ways of tackling the theme with which we are concerned. However, the way which will be followed has not been arbitrarily chosen.

In the first place we must acknowledge the logical priority of the historical fact of the people of Israel, which is the primary reference of the expression 'people of God' in the Bible. If the people of Israel had not existed, there would have been nothing to give rise to the concept. 'People of God' is a confession made by Israel as to its own nature, its peculiar position among the nations of the earth. Since it is not possible in human affairs to separate 'pure' reality from its interpretation, we may say that Israel does not exist apart from its acknowledgment of itself as the people of God, but that nevertheless that acknowledgment depends upon its empirical and historical existence as a people.

In the second place we must pay special attention to the origins of the people of Israel. Israel arose as a revolutionary movement among the peoples who inhabited the land they called Canaan, and which subsequently came to be known as Palestine. When we say that Israel began as a revolution, we mean that its founders were conscious of creating something new in history, with all the qualifications which may be necessary in view of the relative lack of a historical consciousness among the people of the thirteenth century B.C. as compared with those of the twentieth century A.D. A people which owes its existence to a revolutionary exploit will need to justify any new initiatives in the future by reference to the origins which marked it out as a peculiar people. It will have to engage in re-interpretations of the revolutionary exploit in order to legitimise the new directions which national life may be taking. The moment of its foundation will always hold a privileged place in its self-understanding. This is why we believe it to be right that, after giving the historical reality priority over interpretations of it, we should go on to give the moment of its origin priority over subsequent historical developments.

1. ISRAEL, A PEASANT MOVEMENT (*UN MOVIMIENTO COMPESINO*) AS THE PEOPLE OF YAHWEH

Israel came into being in the thirteenth and twelfth centuries B.C. as a result of the gradual unification of a series of peasant uprisings within Canaanite society. From the point of view of our modern social sciences, it was a revolutionary movement of country-dwellers against the domination of the cities, whose life was centred on the monarchical administration. The kings of Canaan, like those of Egypt and Mesopotamia, maintained the military, administrative and religious systems in their capital cities by means of the tribute they exacted from the country villages in which the majority of the population lived. The Bible gives a description of this system in narrative form in Genesis 47:13–26, where it is 'explained' how the whole people of Egypt came to be slaves of Pharaoh, and how he came to be the owner of all the land in the country. Although today we may doubt whether all this came about as the direct result of a famine, in the way it is described in Genesis, the social picture given in the passage is true to reality as it was in Egypt and also in Canaan.

By the fourteenth century B.C. Egypt had begun to lose its control over the minor kings of Canaan who had formerly been subject to it. The diplomatic correspondence of Tel-el-amarna includes many letters addressed to the Egyptian court by kings who claim to be loyal to Egypt and who ask for military help to resist the threat of the 'apiru. Investigations have shown that these 'apiru were rebels of all kinds, and not a single homogeneous group, and that the term was used over a widespread area of the Near East to indicate rebel groups which had no links with each other. The Canaanite movements of 'apiru in the fourteenth century are the immediate precursors of the peasant risings which brought together the tribes of Israel (who were also called Hebrews, a term linguistically parallel to 'apiru).[1]

During the thirteenth century the use of iron was spreading throughout Canaan, and this had a great impact because it made possible the cultivation of mountainous land which had previously been left to grow wild. These previously unprofitable lands were in the mountains, while the kings' cities were for the most part on the more fertile plains. The combination of the weakness of the Egyptian imperial power and the technological advance in agricultural implements explains why, in the course of the fourteenth, thirteenth and twelfth centuries, a series of peasant insurrections took place throughout Canaan, from Galilee in the north to the Arabah in the south. These insurrections brought about the destruction of various cities, and a displacement of the population from the plains to the mountains, which were cleared and populated by peasants who came fleeing from the areas controlled by the kings. Traditions about their battles against the cities are to be found in the books of Joshua and Judges, set within the editorial framework of an invasion and conquest which probably never took place.[2] Some of the groups in the central mountains began to call themselves Israel, a name subsequently adopted by all these groups. Their organisation was typically rural, by families, clans and tribes, in which the assembly of the most respected patriarchs (the elders) took decisions for the whole people.[3]

These tribes achieved their cohesion over a period of several generations by their adherence to the god Yahweh, who was believed to have liberated a 'Hebrew' group from their condition as peasants in servitude to the king of Egypt. The Song of Deborah (Judges 5), an eleventh century poem and perhaps the oldest text in the Bible, reflects an advanced stage in this process. The northern tribes of Galilee and those of the central massif of the mountains of Ephraim waged war in the name of Yahweh against the inhabitants of the cities in the valley separating them. The existence of tribes of Yahweh in Transjordan is recognised, but these took no part in the war. The horizon of the tribes of Yahweh does not extend as far south as what will later become the important tribe of Judah. But it can already be seen, in this ancient poem, that the tribes of Israel are those which acknowledge Yahweh, the God of the Exodus, as their king and god.

At the beginning, then, the 'people of Yahweh' is the collection of peasant tribes living in the mountains of Canaan and refusing to pay tribute to the kings of the cities. Everything suggests that the insurrections preceded both the coming together of the movement into a single 'Israel' and the confession of Yahweh as their god. The latter point is supported by the fact that they called themselves 'Israel'—a theophoric name incorporating the name of the god El, an important god whom we know through the myths contained in the Ugaritic tablets. It comes from a stage prior to the movement's adoption of Yahweh as its god. How then did the peasant tribes of Canaan come to accept Yahweh as their god and to regard themselves as the People of Yahweh? The 'official' answer to this question is to be found in the story of the Exodus: Israel acknowledged Yahweh as its only god because he had liberated them from servitude to the king of Egypt.

The Exodus is the official account of the origins of Israel, and the original revelation of its god, Yahweh. Israel acknowledges Yahweh as its god because Yahweh is the god of the peasants (*campesinos*), the god who waged war against the most powerful king of those times, so that the peasants might escape from Egypt and go in search of a land flowing with milk and honey. Canaanite religion, with such gods as El, Baal, Asherah and Anath, was practised in sanctuaries in the cities of Canaan, under the patronage of their kings. It was part of the system of oppression. But it is very rare for a peasant insurrection to be atheistic, and there is no evidence that Israel ever was. Before coming to know Yahweh, they worshipped the same Canaanite gods that their fathers had known, particularly Baal, who, they believed, gave them the rain in due season. But the most sacred places of the cult of Baal were in the hands of priests who formed part of the royal officials of the towns. The experience of the peasant rebels in Egypt was different. They staged their revolution under the inspiration of Yahweh, a god whom the king and his officials did not know, and were led by Moses, the prophet of Yahweh. Their religion, then, was an exclusively peasant one, with a god who had nothing to do with the official religions of the oppressors.

The above is a probable reconstruction of the origins of Israel, and the way in which Israel came to regard itself as the people of Yahweh. It is based in large measure on the book of Exodus. The text of Exodus is the result of a series of re-interpretations of Israel's origins, made from different historical standpoints. Such re-interpretations are perfectly natural in the development of any people which reviews its origins in the light of changed circumstances. Beginning as the story of the rebellion of some Hebrews against the monarchy, it came to be the story of the rebellion of the tribes of Israel against the monarchy. When Israel came to have its own kings, the ideologists at court turned the story into that of a struggle for national liberation, a struggle by Israelites against Egyptians. After the Exile, when Israel became a nation governed by priests, the Exodus was changed into an occasion for Yahweh to demonstrate that he was the only true god, mocking Pharaoh and his magicians by means of wonders and miracles.[4] The stories of the liberation of the peasants in Canaan underwent an even more drastic transformation. They were changed into an account of the invasion of the land by an already-existing Israel, coming from the desert, and their conquest of what was to be their national homeland. The reconstruction of the origins of Israel which we have sketched out here is the most probable among those suggested by exegetes. Theologically, it enables us to explain the significance of Israel's recognition of itself as the People of Yahweh. Its relationship with Yahweh was marked by an exclusiveness ('Yahweh is a jealous god') which we find reflected in the commandment not to worship other gods. This exclusiveness can be explained in the light of the class struggle at the time of Israel's origin, when Yahweh was the god of the peasants and the enemy of the gods of the kings who exacted tribute from the peasants.

In spite of the fact that its god was the god of a social class, Israel acknowledged a resemblance between its own relationship with Yahweh and that of Sidon with Astarte, or Moab with Chemosh, or Ammon with Milcom (1 Kings 11:33). Yahweh was the national god of Israel. However, neither Astarte nor Chemosh nor Milcom demanded an exclusive loyalty from their worshippers. They were not gods of the poor. Later Yahweh too, like any other national god, became the god of all Israelites, including its kings. But the

Exodus narrative kept alive the memory that Yahweh was the god of the poor. In every generation, Yahweh's prophets pronounced judgment on the kings in the name of the God of the Exodus. Within the monarchy of Israel, the two conceptions of Yahweh found themselves in conflict when the prophet Ahijah persuaded Jeroboam to rebel against Solomon, who was building a temple for Yahweh with the forced labour of Israelite peasants (1 Kings 11:26–40; 12:1–19).

2. ISRAEL AS THE MISSIONARY PEOPLE OF GOD

Although Yahweh was a different kind of national god from Chemosh or Milcom, he was only God in Israel. His nature as god of (all) the poor was in tension with this limitation. From early on, various attempts were made to resolve the tension. The theology of the *convenant* in the seventh century was an attempt to find a theological justification for the election of Israel as the special people of Yahweh. We shall not go into this in depth, but we must look at some of the ways in which the people of Yahweh is given a missionary character.

In an important passage, the Yahwist part of the Pentateuch puts these words into the mouth of Yahweh:

I will make of you a great nation, and I will bless you and make your name great, so that you will be a blessing. I will bless those who bless you, and him who curses you I will curse; and by you all the families of the earth shall bless themselves (Genesis 12:2, 3).

This signified a mission for the people of Yahweh, personified in the partiarch Abraham. The promise is later repeated to Jacob:

Your descendants shall be like the dust of the earth, and you shall spread abroad to the west and to the east and to the north and to the south; and by you and your descendants shall all the families of the earth bless themselves (Genesis 28:14).

What does it mean to the Yahwist that Israel is to spread and be a blessing for the whole earth? Later on in the Yahwist narrative some examples are given: Joseph in Egypt saves the Egyptians from the seven years of famine by having granaries built to store supplies before the famine comes; Pharaoh asks Moses to get the Israelites to pray for him when they hold their feast for Yahweh in the desert (Exodus 8:28; 10:17); the blessings of Balaam, the non-Israelite prophet, who declares that Israel will exercise dominion over many peoples, are especially clear (Numbers 24:3–9, 15–19). It is probable therefore that the Yahwist, writing during the expansionist period of David and Solomon, sees the extension of the rule of the Israelite monarchs (their imperialism) as an extension of the blessings of Yahweh to the nations. There is nothing strange in this, if we remember how the Spaniards saw the conquest of America as a mission to evangelise the Indians, and how the English saw their rule in Asia and Africa as a civilising mission for the benefit of the backward peoples of those territories. The idea of the blessing, then, is in part a justification for David's expansionism, and a concealment of other motives. This is not, however, to deny that, like the modern examples, it contains an element of truth.

We must ask why the second great tradition in the Pentateuch used the generic name God (*Elohim*) in place of the proper name Yahweh. Of course the Elohist tradition is faithful to history in recording that the name Yahweh began to be used only from the time of the Exodus. The Elohist makes this clear as he tells how Yahweh revealed to Moses his previously unknown name (Exodus 3:14–15). The striking thing is that for the god of the patriarchs this tradition avoids the use of any name whatever, but employs the generic plural *elohim* as a grammatical singular. Even after the revelation of the name Yahweh, the Elohist continues to show a preference for the generic name 'God'. In this tradition, Israel begins to see itself as the people of 'God', the universal God, though it knows him in his own intimate nature through his work of liberation in the Exodus. The universality of God can be seen in some characteristic stories, like that of his protection of the Egyptian woman Hagar and her son Ishmael, ancestor of the Arabs (Genesis 21:8–21), or of his positive attitude towards Jethro the Midianite, father-in-law of Moses (Exodus 18), or of God's protection of Abimelech, king of Gerar, by means of a revelation which warned him not to be trapped into adultery by Abraham's deception (Genesis 20:6–7), or of Abraham's pact with Abimelech (Genesis 21:22–34). This interest in non-Israelites is not the paternalism we found in the Yahwist tradition. Such a universal interest is not unconnected with the inclination to eliminate the particularity implied in the use of the name Yahweh for the God of Israel.

The great prophets of Israel took further this awareness that Yahweh was more than the god of Israel. For Amos, Yahweh is the god of the poor, who upholds justice, and who therefore not only delivered Israel from Egypt, but also the Philistines from Caphtor and the Syrians from Kir (Amos 9:7). A prophecy in Isaiah 19:25 foretells the coming of the day when Yahweh will say: 'Blessed be Egypt my people, and Assyria the work of my hands, and Israel my heritage.' Isaiah looks forward to the day when the nations will come to Zion to enquire about the law of Yahweh, and will turn their swords into ploughshares and their spears into pruning-hooks (Isaiah 2:1–5). In Isaiah 10:5–15 the prophet interprets the conquests of Assyria as the result of Yahweh's command to them to rule over the nations. Amos too understands that Yahweh is the Lord of all the nations (Amos 1, 2). Along the same lines, Jeremiah understands that in his generation Yahweh is bringing all the nations under the power of the king of Babylon (Jeremiah 27). In these and other ways, the prophets of Israel show that Yahweh is the only God of the whole of history. This involves a relativisation of the place of Israel in history, a recognition that it cannot cease to be one people among others, although it has had the privilege of being the object of the liberating and self-revealing grace of Yahweh, in the Exodus and on Mount Sinai. If Yahweh is the God of all the world, then Israel's calling itself the People of God acquires a missionary significance.

It is Second Isaiah who draws out the implications of the recognition that Yahweh is the only true God. There are various kinds of implication: Other gods are no more than vanity, and those who worship them are fools (Isaiah 40:18–20; 41:6–7; 45:14–19); Yahweh controls the whole of history, and can perfectly well take hold of the Persian king Cyrus and make the nations of the earth submit to him (Isaiah 41:1–5; 45:1–7); and Israel, the servant of Yahweh, has the mission of making justice and right known in all the earth (Isaiah 42:1–4). Without any show of power, Israel will be a light for the nations.

We have gone over various stages in Israel's consciousness of being the People of God:

(a) In the first instance, Israel is the people of Yahweh because it is the people composed of those whom Yahweh has rescued from servitude in Egypt (and in Canaan).

(b) During the reigns of David and Solomon, Israel becomes the people blessed by Yahweh so that it may bestow on other nations the benefits of its rule.

(c) The Elohist tradition in the Pentateuch thinks of Yahweh simply as God, who blesses Israel in particular, but does not forget the poor of other peoples, like, for example, the Egyptian servant-girl Hagar.

(d) The prophets recognise Yahweh as the Lord of all the nations. This limits the privileges of Israel, whose relationship with Yahweh is dependent upon its observance of justice (Amos).

(e) When, with Jeremiah and Deutero-Isaiah, there comes full recognition that there is only one God, and that the gods of the peoples are only vanity, then it is affirmed that God has chosen the people of Israel to rule over the nations in order that they may come to a knowledge of the true God.

1. JESUS ESTABLISHES A NEW PEOPLE OF GOD, IN VIEW OF THE IMMINENCE OF THE KINGDOM OF GOD

Mark sums up the mission of Jesus in this way: 'Now after John was arrested, Jesus came into Galilee, preaching the gospel of God, and saying, "The time is fulfilled, and the Kingdom of God is at hand; repent, and believe in the gospel" ' (Mark 1:14–15). There is almost unanimous agreement among exegetes that the Kingdom of God was at the heart of the message and the practice of Jesus. Essentially Jesus spoke of nothing else. The Kingdom was the precious pearl for which the merchant sold all his possessions (Matthew 13:45–46). Jesus believed that the Kingdom of God had become a present reality in his own healing ministry and that of his disciples (Luke 11:20; 17:20–21). And he affirmed that the coming of the Kingdom of God in its fulness was so imminent that some members of his own generation would see it (Mark 9:1).

In speaking of the Kingdom of God, Jesus took up a long tradition going back to the peasant revolt, when all monarchies were rejected on the grounds that they were forms of slavery for the peasants. Because he was loyal to the rule of Yahweh, Gideon refused the invitation to be king of Israel (Judges 8:22–23). The story of Jotham is a scathing satire on the kings of the world (Judges 9:7–15). And, according to tradition, the prophet Samuel regarded the insistent desire of Israel to have kings 'like the nations' as a rebellion against Yahweh which could only end in slavery (1 Sam. 8:4–18). We do not know, of course, how far Jesus took account of this biblical tradition, which in some measure was known to all the Jews, if only through those prophecies which foretold the coming of a good king, the Messiah, who would take back the sovereignty usurped by human kings and restore the true Kingdom of God.

The consistent practice of Jesus was not to speak of the Kingdom of God literally, but in parables and similes. It would seem that he had two reasons for this. On the one hand, he did not want to give his enemies the opportunity of using against him something 'heretical' he might have said. On the other hand, he wanted to turn people's attention away from his teaching to his actions. It follows from this latter point that we should examine the actions of Jesus in order to understand his conception of the Kingdom, and thereby of the People, of God.

The most obvious thing is that the people who formed the basis of the Kingdom of God were all poor. When a rich man wanted 'to inherit eternal life' Jesus told him to sell all he had, give the proceeds to the poor, and then follow him (Mark 10:17–27). He warned those who might wish to follow him that they would not even have anywhere to lay their head (Luke 9:57–58). The man who asked for permission to go and bury his father was refused it by Jesus (Luke 9:59–62). Such austerity imposed on the followers of Jesus confirms and interprets the teaching that the Gospel is for the poor (Luke 4:18; 7:22).

In this 'people of the Kingdom', all would be brothers, without titles or distinctions (Matthew 23:8–10). The natural family had to be left behind, since the family too might serve as a place of refuge where a person would forget the primacy of the people made up of those who do the will of the Father (Mark 3:31–35). Being a disciple of Jesus meant hating one's father, mother, wife and children (Luke 14:25–26). The places of importance in this new people would not be allocated as in the nations of the world, where the great are the ones who exercise authority over the rest. Rather the greatest would be the one who rendered most service to the rest (Mark 10:41–45).

After the death of Jesus, a significant group of his followers set up a community in Jerusalem, to continue in an urban context the movement Jesus had begun in his wandering ministry. In order to do it, those who had property sold it and brought the proceeds to the apostles. In this way no-one suffered hardship, since distribution was made to the poor according to their need (Acts 2:43–47; 4:32–37).

Paul understood the mission of Jesus Christ as an act of solidarity with the poor, so that by means of the poverty of the Son of God the poor might become rich (2 Cor. 8:9; Phil. 2:5–11). Within the people made up of those who called themselves by the name of Christ, each person had the duty of bearing the burdens of the others (Gal. 6:2–3). There should be no distinctions or privileges in this new humanity. Jew and Gentile, slave and free man, male and female were one single entity in Christ Jesus (Galatians 3:28). The letter to Philemon, the privileges enjoyed by some members of the church in Corinth, and the condemnation of respect of persons in the letter of James all show that this new style of community was easier to describe than to live out. However, in spite of its faults, this new people was formed on the model provided by the practice of Jesus and his disciples, the model presented to us in those books of recollections which we call the four gospels.

What can we say then? The starting-point in the Bible was the revolutionary peasant movement which rejected the dominant class in antiquity, the king and his court. These people called themselves the people of Yahweh, because they knew Yahweh as the god who had set them free from slavery by overthrowing the powerful king of Egypt. At another point in history, Jesus took up the conviction that it was possible to establish the Kingdom of God on earth. He did not talk in terms of a homogeneous peasant-class, nor of a clearly-defined class-enemy, but rather called on people of all classes in Palestine to live in community and equality, assuring them that the power of the God of their ancestors had performed, and would perform, mighty works among them.

Translated by G. W. S. Knowles

Notes

1. Much has been written about the '*apiru*. A recent valuable work is Marvin L. Chaney 'Ancient Palestinian Peasant Movements and the Formation of Premonarchic Israel' in *Palestine in Transition: The Emergence of Ancient Israel* ed. David Noel Freedman and David Frank Graf (Sheffield 1983) pp. 39–94.

2. Jorge Pixley 'La toma de la tierra de Canaán: ¿ liberación o despojo?' in *Taller de Teología* 12 (1983) 5–14.

3. Norman K. Gottwald *The Tribes of Yahweh: A Sociology of the Religion of Liberated Israel, 1250–1050 B.C.* (Maryknoll, 1979). This work contains a full discussion of the social organisation of Israel in its earliest days.

4. A commentary on Exodus which recognises the importance of the re-interpretations of the story is that by Jorge Pixley *Exodo: una lectura evangélica y popular* (Mexico 1983).

Giuseppe Alberigo

The People of God (*le Popolo di Dio*) in the Experience of Faith

IN THE early Church, what made Christians 'other' in relation to non-Christians was the embodiment of their faith in Christ in baptism and participation in the eucharist. They were Christians, that is, People of God, by virtue of this alone; no other historical or social condition or situation affected the matter (see Gal. 3:27–8). This was not only true in relation to non-Christians; it was true within the Church as well: any service, any authority, any charism, even the special participation of the bishop in the unique priesthood of Christ, did not make their holders more Christian, did not separate them from the common condition of Christians, did not confer any privileges on those invested with them. The active existence of a plurality of ministries (see 1 Cor. 12:4–11; 14:24), nearly always temporary, it should be realised, must be seen against the fact that whatever gift was received, whatever function exercised, what was permanent and set apart was the fact of being Christian. No less clear is the conviction that from this point of view there is only one hierarchy: that of holiness (1 Cor 12:31, 13), in which all Christians are 'disciples' of the one Lord and 'brothers' one of another.

Christians lived in this basic unity, with the inner structure of a plurality of ministers, in each individual church, united round the Pasch of the Lord, the inexhaustible complexity of the Christian mystery, which is partially and in a complementary fashion revealed in each of the churches. Awaiting the consummation of this mystery, each church lived the communion of love between all its members. And in the same spirit of waiting, each church, summoned by the Spirit in a particular place, knew itself called to live the essence of the New Alliance in its eucharistic community, as an authentic anticipation of the Kingdom, knowing too that the fraternal communion of all the churches could result in the Church becoming the people chosen and called together by God, the body of Christ in the mystery of his relationship of love with the Father and the Spirit.

The eschatological tension always present in the apostolic Church drew attention away from the consequences of adopting certain existing linguistic and social models, whose influence and conditioning became progressively stronger with the historical and social stabilising of the Christian community. Today, with the benefit of hindsight, it is not difficult to see how, particularly in those areas most strongly influenced by Judaism, the Hebraic religious tradition exerted a powerful influence, seen in the separation of a priestly caste. This separation was based partly on the 'sacred' nature of worship and perhaps a very literal understanding of the relationship between the Creator and creation, and partly on the theological concept of the 'remnant of Israel', identified with the priestly caste itself. The strength of this tradition influenced the tendency in some Christian communities to reintroduce a separate priestly caste within their church (the 'new Israel'), thereby weakening the basic unity of the People of God.

Nevertheless, the distinction soon introduced into Christian speech between *clerics* and *laity* was not at first taken as something rigid and permanent, nor were its effects mutually exclusive, as can be seen from the ecclesiastical function reserved to the Emperor (even if this was a woman), or the theological *magisterium* exercised by a layman such as Origen.[1] These are not exceptional cases, but typical facts that exemplify a general situation. In different ways and to different degrees the whole Christian people took part, in the first centuries, in the sacramental activities of the Church, particularly in the sacraments of penance and the eucharist.[2] The exclusion of the bulk of the people from this participation came about only in the fourth century, along with the distinction brought about in architectural terms between the zone of the altar and the body of the church reserved for the faithful.[3]

The more properly ministerial-hierarchic aspect of guiding the community was also characterised absolutely by the lack of any definite separation between clerics and lay people. Ordination in the first place did not express just the insertion of the new cleric into a body of clergy (the concept of *ordo* came only later), but the assignation to him of an office within the community, which at the same time expressed a special participation in the priesthood of Christ. The most significant aspect of this fact is that the indelible character of ordination was recognised only in the fourth century.

Another pointer to the high degree in which the people participated in responsiblity for the community is of course the choice of ministers. It was not the priestly caste that generated its new members from within its own ranks, setting them apart from the people, but the community acting as a whole that chose those responsible for its own guidance. This is so well known that it can easily be forgotten and needs to be stressed: think of the election of Ambrose, and Cyprian's affirmation on the participation of the people, on the votes of the faithful as an essential element for the validity of the election of a bishop—the widespread equivalence between the terms 'election' and 'consecration' in the early centuries is itself highly significant.

Effectively, the only distinction that mattered was between Church and world, the thrust of which was to inspire the whole People of God with an evangelising and missionary zeal. Each community was at once a segment and a sacramental dimension of the one people of believers working in history in the search for and building up of the Kingdom.

Between the fourth and fifth centuries, the Christian Church underwent deep changes, not only numerically. The numbers of baptised and of communities increased enormously; Christians were present in all social circles and in all departments of life; the ending of persecution weakened the eschatological expectation and the feeling of being 'strangers' in society. All these changes also had effects within the structure of the People of God. The distinction, for example, between 'precepts'—binding on all the baptised—and 'counsels'—binding only on some—was now formulated and gradually accepted.[4] This helped the emergence of the view of monasticism as a *tertium genus* between clergy and laity; monastic charism and experience developed into the '*ordo monachorum*'. The division of Christians into categories (*doctores, contemplativi, coniugati*) also came about at this time, through an Augustinian reading of the New and Old Testaments, which perhaps also reflected the increasingly marked categorisations coming into use in civil society (*oratores, bellatores, laborantes*). A categorisation to which, it should be noted, Augustine himself attributed a purely descriptive and not intrinsic meaning, in no way designed to indicate a moral hierarchy of states of life.[5]

Another important factor was the setting-up, particularly in the West, of a very extensive ecclesiastical organisation, which became a major centre of authority and power, control of which brought very definite political and economic advantages. The whole structure became an object of contention between those who controlled it and those who would have liked to control it; thus there came into being an 'eccelsiastical' structure which—depending on one's point of view—should be reserved to the 'clergy' or open to the 'laity'.

Once the Church received a statute in the public jurisprudence of the Empire, not only was its structure affected, but the role and place of Christians also underwent significant changes. At the time of Constantine, Christians became eligible to hold office in the civil administration and this 'establishment' of Christians in society had far-reaching consequences. Futhermore, the mass entry of pagans into the Church brought about a lessening of fervour and a certain worldliness crept into Christian life. This had the effect of a levelling-out between ordinary Christians and the people *tout court*, of which significant indicators are the disappearance of the catechumenate and the married diaconate and lowering of the age for the administration of baptism. This weakening of the Church-world opposition led—as both consequence and reaction at the same time—to a 'strict' definition of the Church, which became identified with the 'clergy' and the 'sacred'.

With the passage of time and in the interests of 'order', the dynamic plurality of ministries and charisms within the Church was gradually extinguished, giving way to a single form of priestly ministry, progressively seen as permanent, exclusive (non-participatory), set apart (no labour, no family). The advent of barbarism throughout Europe which followed the overthrow of the Roman Empire in the West, from which only islands of monasticism and the schools attached to the cathedrals escaped, meant that non-clerical Christians lost any possibility of taking an active and productive part in religious thinking; learning became a factor for discrimination among the baptised.

The feudal ordering of Christian society between the sixth and tenth centuries accentuated the tendency to emphasise divisions and specialisations within the Church as well às in civil society, pushing consciousness of its unity into second place. Duly hierarchised differentiations were seen as more important than unity; the Church was no longer represented horizontally as a communion of sister communities, but vertically, as a pyramid.[6]

The setting-up of these strata and their predominance over the basic unity of the Christian condition lasted into the Low Middle Ages, during which elements already present, but in embryonic and fluctuating form, in the preceding centuries, came to maturity. The historical scene in which this came about was dominated by demands for reform and purification of the Church, but also by an ever-increasing degree of authority reserved to the juridical side of the ecclesiastical establishment, by a highly systematic theology, strongly allied to an exact social philosophy, and by a tendency to emphasise the static aspects of the social fabric at the expense of its dynamic ones. From this background, several decisive aspects emerge. The first is the prevalence of a concept of the Church—on both doctrinal and practical levels—in which hierarchy is the dominant value, and in which, therefore, the *universitas fidelium* becomes the passive and subject base of a complex hierarchical pyramid, whose active levels are made up of the clergy, with the pope at the apex. Significantly, this was the time when the Church applied to itself the secular differentiation of men into *genera* and *ordines*, as witness so many theological and canonical texts of the twelfth and thirteenth centuries, culminating in Gratian's significant and well-known saying: *Duo sunt genera christianorum*.[7] According to this text, there are two well defined and quite separate *genera*: the *ordo clericorum* and the *ordo laicorum*, to which some would add a third, the *ordo monachorum* (though this was by now made up exclusively of clerics); these 'orders' formed increasingly mutually exclusive worlds, impenetrable to outsiders.

The continued growth of ecclesiastical wealth led at this time to the increasing autonomy of the *ordo clericorum*, to whom the availability and use of this wealth were guaranteed in rigorously exclusive fashion. For a time it seemed as though this state of affairs was to be critically threatened by the foundation, in the early thirteenth century, of the mendicant Orders, with their enormous popular support. But in fact, at least by the time the first generation had been superseded by the second, the Mendicants accepted complete clericalisation, with the single exception of being exempt from the rule of the local bishop.

The most significant manifestation of this development seems to lie in a basic Christian anthropology of dualist tenor, according to which the division of Christians into *genera* is not only obvious and rigid, but corresponds to the distinction between heaven and earth, not to mention that between the spiritual and the carnal, with an explicit and immediate moral implication that owes more to Stoicism than to Pauline theology. Indicative of this approach is the Prologue to the *Summa* of Stephen of Tournai, which proclaims: 'Civitas Ecclesia, civitatis rex Christus, duo populi in Ecclesia, duo ordines clericorum et laicorum; duo vitae, spiritualis et carnalis . . .' Now everthing is ready for the different *ordines* to be given different Christian values.[8] The biblical reality of the People of God no longer suffices to describe a Church so jealous of its internal distinctions and sufficiently integrated in society to be able to pursue the mirage of a Christian society, 'Christendom'.[9]

Several attempts were made to reverse this tendency. On the one hand, the popular medieval heresies opposed the legal equation 'cleric = first-class Christian' with the factual statement 'cleric = wicked Christian', invoking an *ecclesia spiritualis*, in which juridical structures and the priestly ministry would be radically eliminated, or at least substantially reduced. On the other hand, there were the great organisational phenomena of ordinary Christians forming Confraternities and Third Orders. These were movements which substantially accepted the existing state of affairs, seeking to obtain—through a share in the great spiritual privileges extended to the Mendicants in particular—an assimilation, even if only partial, to the condition of objective advantage which the *clerici* had obtained for themselves. Thus there came into being the first attempts at what was later to become known as 'lay advancement', basically aimed at sharing in some measure in the clerical life and thereby gaining a certain share in clerical privileges (one thinks of all the canonical legislation in favour of the Oratories and the exemptions granted to Confraternities).

The thirteenth and fourteenth centuries saw a number of more interesting attempts, in that they expressed the desire of groups, sometimes very numerous, of ordinary Christians to achieve an effective stake in the life of the Church and the responsiblities inherent in it, thereby overcoming their condition of second-class Christians, their purely passive and consumerist position and—furthermore—the attitude of rivalry between different groups, which had come into being. Great religious manifestations such as the Confraternities of the 'Whites' or the 'Battuti' or the *Devotio moderna* were all efforts to stress, in the first place through personal endeavour realised in communion with the brethren, the authenticity of a non-clerical Christian condition, with no diminishment of capacity for the *imitatio Christi*. In these circles, great stress was laid on the ecclesial vocation of every Christian as a response to a call from God, a vocation whose fulness is measured exclusively by the degree of generosity and fidelity in the response itself. In the event, however, after having won a very widespread following, these movements found themselves in an unfavourable climate in the Church, and were finally pushed to the periphery when the reaction against Protestantism led the whole of the Church that remained in communion with Rome to choose the path of an intransigent defence of late-medieval ecclesiology allied to the zeal of Bellarmine.[10]

Defence of the authenticity of the ministerial priesthood, of the 'religious life' (which is no longer synonymous with Christian life, but only with life according to the 'counsels'), and a response to the Protestant affirmation of the common priesthood of all Christians, seemed possible only through a massive reaffirmation of the objective condition of privilege attaching to the clerical caste, though this was now tied to a new strictness in moral life. The adversarial tendency of theology in the decades following the Reformation, and succeeding centuries, meant that any serious examination of the deep, providential meaning of Protestant theses on the common Christian condition became progressively more impossible.

The Tridentine canons, actually quite sober in their wording, were for centuries read from the standpoint of a Church in which the Christian people were quite simply a corollary of the hierarchy. The definition of the Church in a strict sense, beginning to gain ground, acquired ever more exclusive overtones, so that *ecclesial* and *ecclesiastical* became synonymous, and finally the latter took the place of and completely eclipsed the former. The decisive significance of baptism was greatly weakened, largely because of the existence of a diversity of Christian churches, and an individualistic appreciation of the mass and the eucharist on one hand, and of disciplinary structures on the other, gained ground. Salvation came to be sought less and less through the *ecclesia*, as the community of the baptised, and more and move through an individual religious relationship mediated through the priesthood. Christian life and ecclesial life became steadily less synonymous and the moral aspect of Christianity took on an extraordinary importance; 'charity' and 'mission' were understood in an increasingly philanthropic sense. The clerical monopoly on theological thinking was consolidated, and all non-moral dimensions of Christianity became generally accepted as 'priests' affairs', both by clericalists and by anti-clericalists. The existence of a 'clerical caste' became not only a social and cultural fact, a matter of habit and mentality, but something sanctioned not only by canon law, but also by modern States—ecclesiastics are exempt from civil prosecution, from taxes, from military service, etc. . . .

Other major features of the modern age conspired to deepen the doctrinal and actual separation between ordinary Christians and the clergy. The first aspect to note was the improvement in the morals of the Catholic clergy brought about by the Council of Trent, especially through the example and work of the new Company of Jesus and the other new Orders and Congregations, and through the institution of seminaries, a development which had the effect of deepening the rift between the priesthood and the common Christian condition by giving an exalted status to the clergy as a Christian caste set apart, a citadel of Christian life to which were ceded, either devolved as of right or usurped through weakness, the prerogatives and obligations that should have belonged to all Christians.

Besides this, various illuminist circles in seventeenth-century Europe made increasingly pressing efforts to emphasise the existence and legitimacy of non-clerical, or a-clerical, and finally anti-clerical Christianity. Though their efforts were based on a thin doctrinal content, they showed themselves capable of arousing wide, and therefore significant support, for their denunciation of the divorce between the clergy and the Church, presented, it must be said, in positive terms.

The centuries of the modern age have seen a progressive mutual estrangement between Christianity and the world, both on the level of thought and culture, and on that of everyday life of the common people. Such a state of affairs was long ascribed to the progress of evil (de-Christianisation), from a standpoint that can only be described as inert and only nominally Christian. Faced with the continual dimunition of the sphere of 'good', a substantially passive attitude was adopted, challenging and protesting about the way things were going, but without finding the energy to turn back the tide. So any initiative that proposed a Christian response based on a global consideration of the real state of the Church generally met with an attitude of instinctive distrustfulness. Two sides of Christianity continued on their way: one aristocratic, learned, speaking Latin; the other an affair of processions, cults of the Saints, passive and inert attendance at mass; the moment was drawing near when Christianity had to face up to a practical return of paganism.

In the face of this, the Church, reduced with each succeeding generation to an even narrower sphere, became ever more strictly an 'affair of the priests', to the point where such an unusual historical conjuncture became a permanent structural situation.[11] That is, the reduction of the Church to the clergy (and later to the hierarchy alone) became accepted, with the 'simple faithful' being implored to remain true to the faith of their fathers (and in the end to Christ) through increasingly narrow and clericalised channels, while the rest of humanity—non-Catholic Christians and 'others', even if baptised, were condemned to perdition *en masse*.

The acceptance of such a state of affairs brought with it an increasing emphasis on the juridical-institutional aspect of the Church, in whose favour an uninterrupted displacement of the axis of the Church's life and of its very conception of itself insensibly occurred. The marginalisation of the sacramental dimension became evident even within priestly circles with the granting of hierarchical authority to cardinals and members of the Roman Curia, totally independently of their participation in the priestly or episcopal ministries. A significant factor in this direction has been the clerical staffing of every ecclesiastical 'office', however materially concerned and irrelevant to a priestly ministry these might be.

Vatican I can be seen as the culminating point of this phase: the two decrees it approved sanctioned respectively the privilege of *infallibility* for the Hierarchy, and the duty of *faith* for Christians.

The isolation of the Church can be seen to have become ever more acute as a result of the growth of mass political and social movements in the nineteenth century. This led to a spontaneous mobilisation of the Catholic laity in Europe in an attempt to overcome the deep estrangement of the Church from the problems of the time, particularly in the social sphere. Lay Catholic organisations all moved in the direction of lively social, and therefore also inevitably political, endeavour.

Catholic Action as a form of collaboration in the hierarchical apostolate[12] was the reassertion of the total dependence of any lay movement on the clerical caste: lay people were accepted as indispensable collaborators from the moment when the shortage of vocations meant that the clergy could no longer be self-sufficient, and from the moment when society seemed to refuse to give ever greater devotion to and place ever greater trust in the clerical habit.[13]

The laity became a sort of assault battalion, the Church's shock troops. The Church's dependence on them in this role, however, still excluded them from any share in the theological or thinking function of the Church. 'Catholic Action is not guiding action in the theoretical sphere, but an executive branch in the practical sphere'.[14] So action became widely seen as the way, virtually the only way open to lay people, of expressing their Christian fervour: each successive atavistic and organisational excess henceforth found adequate justification.[15]

The laity in this way became a band of Christians slipping from anonymity towards clericalisation (para-sacerdotal spirituality: consecrations, vows, used to express not special charisms but the ordinary Christian vocation). The doctrinal dimension of this situation was the theology of the laity (clue: not *by* the laity, but *for* the laity); basically, the dualism between first- and second-class Christians remained intact.

Parallel to this process went the phase of '*consecratio mundi*' as the proper vocation of the laity, the result of a pessimistic view of the relationship between Christianity and the world, seeing 'earthly realities' as in need of a modern dose of Redemption, as though the whole of creation were not already under the sign of the Son of Man. This approach produced great energy in the direction of missionary endeavour, but distorted into a sort of social work *ad extra*, continuing to see the '*res sacrae*', the Church, as the legitimate monopoly of clerics. So there was produced a sort of consensual partition of spheres of influence, as had already been tried in the preceding century.

The interest aroused by both these trends, particularly after the state of inertia in which so much energy had lain fallow for so long, coincided with the increasingly rapid and widespread modification of the class struggle in the shape of a general mobilisation of the traditionally passive levels of society, a lively development of community and association spirit and a theoretical and practical levelling-out of the rights of the individual. The hierarchical aspect of human society, based on privileged conditions not based on merit, was finally giving way before a strong current of egalitarianism, with rank based only on personal merit or social function. Against this background, the Holy Spirit moved to awaken in a large number of Christians a consciousness of a 'time of the Church', time for an effort to rethink the whole ecclesial reality on the basis of the most authentic parts of the New Testament on the one hand, and of major historical indicators, the 'signs of the times', on the other.

The need for such a rethinking was seen in widely different circles and situations, giving rise at the beginning of the present century, and even more intensely in the period between the two World Wars, to a ferment of initiatives on the doctrinal, spiritual and practical planes which today—with the benefit of hindsight—we see as a series of Movements. So there were the Biblical Movement, the Liturgical Movement, the movement of return to early sources, particularly the Fathers, the Missionary Movement, the Ecumenical Movement. A constant characteristic of these experiences was that they brought together Christians of different backgrounds, callings and states of life, on a basis of substantial equality, to address common convictions and endeavours. Such meetings were naturally facilitated by the numerous contacts between clergy and lay people which had taken place in recent decades under the auspices of Catholic Action and various other organisations. The results of this state of affairs gradually came to be seen as widespread and far-reaching, even if ease of contacts and psychological confidence were often only tacked on to a basic attitude of aloofness, in which what separated was concentrated on more than what unites.

At the end of the Second World War the dynamic factors inherent in this situation led to some developments which ofter seemed surprising or aberrant, while—in point of fact—they were consistent with the inner logic of the task assigned, decades earlier, to the whole of Catholic Action. This very rapidly grew in numbers, opening its ranks to include a large band of Christians impelled to do something either by the movement of the Spirit or by the changed historical situation.

On the organisational level, the main result was the formation of a series of 'movements', 'works', 'branches', each with a specialised purpose, the consequence of a sectionalist pastoral outlook which completely lost sight of the basic unity—human and theological—of the People of God, indulging in a drive for effectiveness incompatible with a Church truly seeking to be 'the family of God'. On the structural level, the final end of this was a tendency to make Catholic Action, and particularly its 'cadres', into a parallel Church (more than a 'reserve clergy'), a structure that would duplicate that of the eccelsiastical hierarchy at all levels and tend—by virtue of an immediate relationship with the pope—to obtain a sort of 'exemption' even more divisive than that accorded to monks and friars.

It is becoming clear that in the last century *the age-old division of the Church into 'clergy' and 'laity' was entering its terminal phase as the result of a crisis brought about not only by external challenges, but also by internal contradictions. Both have pointed up the irremediable inadequacy of the 'clergy-laity' dichotomy as an expression of the deep reality of the Church* as seen with the degree of understanding which the Spirit is nourishing in our time.

The brief historical analysis outlined above enables us to shed light on two particularly interesting aspects of the question brought out in some Vatican II texts.

Without going into too much detail, it is worth bearing in mind that two distinct doctrinal currents came together in the conciliar debates:

(1) The first current is the 'theology of the laity', most authoritatively formulated by Yves Congar in his *Jalons pour une théologie du laïcat* in 1952 and by Mgr G. Philips in his *Le Rôle du laïc dans l'Eglise* in 1954, and most effectively demonstrated in the best aspects of Catholic Action. This theology inspired Chapter IV of *Lumen Gentium* and the decree *Apostolicam Actuositatem* in particular, these marking both the acceptance and the high point of achievement of this approach. This, however, has shown itself incapable of moving beyond an essentially negative formulation, and has also extended the 'clergy-laity' polarisation from the individual to the whole of reality, superimposing it on the 'sacred-profane' polarisation and thereby making common cause with the 'theology of earthly realities'. Attempts at a positive definition of 'the laity'[16] have succeeded mainly in showing up the limitations of this approach, which had the merit of stimulating lay appreciation of the question, but cannot really be called a 'theology', basically because of its lack of any foundation either in Revelation or in the Catholic tradition. Furthermore, the question of 'secularisation' has undermined the foundations of the very terminology used in the '*consecratio mundi*'. Today it is clearer than ever that the 'theology of the laity', as would be expected from its origins in an attempt to supplement and 'make do' with regard to the privileges accorded to the clergy, has not been, and could never be, a theology, but only an ideology. It contains numerous fragments of theology, but these can only be properly organised within a true and proper theology of the Church.[17]

(2) '*Sacramental ecclesiology*' was the second doctrinal current influencing the Council, seen above all in Chapter I, II and V of *Lumen Gentium*, but also in many passages of the Constitutions on the Liturgy and on Revelation and in the Decree on Ecumenism. Here we are dealing with a theology directly inspired by Scripture and the apostolic tradition. It has experienced, both in the Catholic world and in all other areas of Christianity, a new spring over the last century and particularly in the last few decades. It has gradually acquired greater depth and vision under the impetus of the Holy Spirit, so that an important stage in its development such as Pius XII'S *Mystici Corporis* of 1943 can today be seen to have been superseded in most respects by the conciliar *magisterium*. The significant aspect of this theology of the Church is that it is the fruit of all those movements of renewal that have flourished in the past few decades, made up indiscriminately of 'clerics' and 'lay people', brought together by a common desire of fidelity simply to being Christian, being Church, the People of God on their way.[18]

It is as well to realise the dual presence of these two different approaches in the complex body of Vatican II. The more so as the first was represented in its final phase, at the end of a long, detailed and worthy effort aimed at reclaiming an active ecclesial status, as opposed to a merely passive and minority one, for at least the most sensitive groups and circles of ordinary Christians, while the second approach was in a phase of youthful dynamism, aiming to mobilise energies and encourage experience of ecclesial life as the full, active and visible communion of all the baptised.

Historically, one could say that *these two approaches are two successive sections of an interrupted line along which modern Christianity has been moving toward an ever fuller understanding of the paschal mystery*. From a doctrinal point of view, however, it is perhaps not prudent to hide the deep truly theological differences that separate the two approaches. Finally, from a practical, operative standpoint, there is no getting away from the fact that while modern lay organisations, and particularly Catholic Action, were, up to the end of the Second World War, often a vehicle for developing an understanding of the Church, since then, and particularly now, they constitute a brake and obstacle to ecclesial understanding, which has flourished on a wider scale under the inspiration of the Spirit and the guidance of the Council.

Today we can see the whole question with new eyes; taking the historical developments of the matter into account, we are blessed with a new freedom to approach the problem through a more vigorous understanding of the mystery of the Church as the People of God. The Christian community as a whole now takes a more urgent view of the need to feel united in a common baptism, hearing of the Word and eucharistic communion. It sees that the participation of each individual Christian and that of the bishop (with his ministers) are different, but that the two priesthoods are in a continual and fruitful dialectical tension. This tension is analogous to that which exists between the ultimate destiny belonging to being Christians (destined to continue even after the end of the Church, in the Kingdom), and the historical elements of the ecclesial condition (destined to finish with the end of the Church, along with the ministerial priesthood). There is an increasingly strong feeling of the need to rediscover, in each local ecclesial community, a space for the charisms and services which the Spirit wishes to inspire and through which (from the deacon-father of a family to the theologian-father of a family and so on) each church, and finally the whole communion of churches, can draw closer in a richer and more varied way to the many-sided mystery of Christ.

If they are to move in this direction, all the baptised, ordinary Christians and members of the episcopal College, should prepare themselves for a task of research and experimentation, for an effort at understanding the present state of affairs and, together, at discovering a way forward. Finally, they need be prepared to renounce an imposed uniformity and the false, though consoling, feeling of security that this gives, in order to undertake a humble, determined, dynamic and faithful search for the ways in which 'the Spirit speaks to the Churches'.

There is a series of critical points on which such an *aggiornamento* of basic attitudes must depend. Such points, to give just some examples, are: the calling and training of the clergy, their way of life, their way of celebrating the liturgy as an act of the whole Church; the whole approach to catechesis, to proclaiming the Word in the Church and to those outside it; recognition and interpretation of the 'signs of the times'. On all these and other such points, whose centrality to the religious life of everyone means that they cannot be subject to any *reservatum ecclesiasticum*, each Church should feel inspired to realise its duty and to exercise its right to make sure that its members undertake the common Christian task of acting responsibly, in a spirit of witness and charity, in community.

In more general terms, the rediscovery of the Church as People of God cannot be limited to feeble enunciations of principle[19], but must call on and reactivate traditional, but long atrophied, aspects if it is really to affect the life of the Church and its ruling structures. The *sensus fidelium* needs to recover a central place among the criteria for the discernment of faith[20], the consensus of the People of God needs to recover an effective influence on the process by which the mind of the Church is formed: reception by the people cannot be a decisive element in verifying the validity of the direction taken by the Churches.

Translated by Paul Burns

Notes

1. See E. Lanne 'Le Laïcat dans l'Eglise ancienne', in *Verbum Caro* 71–2 (1965) 105–126.

2. B. Renaud 'L'Eglise comme assemblée liturgique selon S. Cyprien', in *Recherches de théologie ancienne et médiévale* 38 (1971) 5–68.

3. See Hippolytus 'In Danielem I 17', in *Sources chrétiennes* 14, p. 85.

4. John Chrysostom writes eloquently in the *Adversus oppugnatores vitae monasticae*: 'Nam cum dicit: Venite ad me omnes qui laboratis . . . (Matt. 11:28); non monachis tantum loquitur, sed toti

humano generi. Cumque iubet per angustam incedere viam, non illos modo, sed omnes homines alloquitur'. (PG 47, 374; see also PG 63, 67).

5. See G. Folliet 'Les Trois catégories de chrétiens à partir de Luc (17:34–36), Matthieu (24:40–41) et Ezéchiel (14:14)', in *Augustinus Magister* (Paris 1954) pp. 631–644; *ibid.* 'Les Trois catégories de chrétiens. Survie d'un thème augustinien', in *L'Année théologique augustinienne* 14 (1954) 81–96.

6. Gilbert of Limerick writes in his *De statu ecclesiae*: 'Et tota quidem imago *pyramidis formam* pretendit (Ecclesia) quia inferius ampla est, ubi carnales et coniugatos recipit; superius autem acuta, ubi arctam viam religiosis et ordinatis proponit' (PL 159, 997a).

7. 'Duo sunt genera christianorum. Est autem gens unum, quod mancipatum divino offitio, et deditum contemplationi et orationi, ab omni strepitu temporalium cessare convenit, ut sunt clerici, et Deo devoti, videlicet conversi, κλῆρος enim grece latine sors. Inde huiusmodi homines vocantur clerici, id est sorte electi. Omnes enim Deus in suos elegit. Hi namque sunt reges, id est se et alios regentes in virtutibus, et ita in Deo regnum habent. Et hoc designat corona in capite. Hanc coronam habent ab institutione Romanae ecclesiae in signo regni, quod in Christo expectatur. Rasio vero capitis est temporalium omnium depositio. Illi enim victu et vestitu contenti nullam inter se proprietatem habentes, debent habere omnia communia. Aliud vero est genus Christianorum, ut sunt laici. Λαός enim est populus. His licet temporalia possidere, sed non nisi ad usum. Nihil enim miserius est quam propter nummum Deum contempnere. His concessum est uxorem ducere, terram colere, inter virum et virum iudicare, causas agere, oblationes super altaria ponere, decimas reddere, et ita salvari poterunt, si vicia tamen benefaciendo evitaverint.', c.7 C.XII q.1; ed. Friedberg 678.

8. See *I laici nella 'societas christiana' dei secoli XI e XII* (Milan 1968), esp. the contributions by Y.-M. Congar, L. Prosdocimi and G.-G. Meersseman.

9. 'Forme e problemi attuali della Cristianità', in *Christianesimo nella storia* 5 (1984) 30–180.

10. The *exordium* to the second *Controversy*, devoted to the doctrine of members of the Church, is significant: 'Quid haec nomina Clerici atque laici sibi velint, nemini dubium esse puto: tametsi enim Graecam originem habeant tamen trita sunt, ac per vulgata. Quis enim ignorat idem esse λαόν Graecis, quod populum Latinis? Idem illis, κλῆρ0ν, quod sortem, sive haereditatem nobis? Inde igitur laici dicti sunt quasi plebeii, ac populares, quibus nulla pars functionis Ecclesiasticae demandata est; Clerici autem quasi Domini sors et haereditas, qui divino cultui consecrati, procurandae religionis ac rerum sacrarum, Deo ipso iubente, providentiam, ac solicitudinem susceperunt' *De Controversiis christianae fidei* 11 (Mediolani 1721) 207. Bellarmine is here following a passage from the *Duo sunt genera christianorum*, which he too erroneously attributed to St Jerome.

11. Leo XIII wrote in a letter to the Archbishop of Tours, in December 1888: 'It is, in reality, constant and evident that there are in the Church two naturally well distinct orders: the shepherds and the flock, which means to say the leaders and the people. The first order has the functions of teaching, governing, directing men in their lives, imposing rules; the second has the duty of being subject to the first, of obeying them, of carrying out their orders and rendering them honour.'

12. On the subject of this definition it is useful to remember that Pius XI spoke of 'participation in the hierarchical apostolate', while Pius XII preferred the term 'collaboration', to prevent Catholic Action claiming any true participation in power and authority, that is in the hierarchy's rule. See Pius XII, 'Allocuzione ai dirigenti dell'A.C. Italiana del 3 maggio 1951' in *Discorsi e radiomessagi* XIII, pp. 68–69.

13. See, besides the part of Pius X's encyclical *Il fermo proposito* relating to the relationship between Catholic Action and the hierarchy, Pius XI's letter to Cardinal Cerejeira, Patriarch of Lisbon, 10 November 1933: 'But this (Catholic Action) will not bear its healthy fruits if its members are not formed and guided by experienced directors and above all by good ecclesiastical Assistants, in whose hands primarily rest the fate and destiny of these associations.'

14. Letter from the Cardinal Secretary of State to Cardinal Hlond, Primate of Poland, 10 April 1929.

15. Pius XI speaking to Spanish pilgrims, 22 September 1933: 'Action is the sign of life, of that life brought by God to the world and bought to our profit at the price of his precious blood. Without

action, without movement, without activity there is only death, or at best an empty, sleepy, torpid, useless life; so that Catholic Action is the sign, cause and very measure of life.'

16. Particularly important contributions were articles by K. Rahner on 'L'Apostolat des laïcs' in *Nouv. Rev. Théol.* (1966) 3–33, and Ch. Baumgartner 'Formes diverses de l'apostolat deas laïcs' in *Christus* (1957) 9–33, taken up by Y.-M. Congar in 1957 in 'Esquisse d'une théologie de l'Action Catholique' (in *Sacerdoce et laïcat devant leurs tâches d'évangelisation et de civilisation,* Paris, 1962, pp. 328–356), and again in some pages of self-criticism published as an Appendix to the 3rd edn. of *Jalons . . .,* pp. 648–651. The most recent synthesis is Congar's 'Laïc et laïcat' in DS 9 (1976) 79–108.

17. An interesting and significant witness to the persistence of this approach can be seen in the unfortunate title originally proposed for the future Ch. II of *Lumen Gentium*: 'De populo Dei et speciatim de Laicis'; see *Constitutionis dogmaticae Lumen Gentium Synopsos historica* ed. G. Alberigo & F. Magistretti (Bologna, 1975) pp. 43 and 163.

18. See the excellent piece by O. Semmelroth 'The Church, new People of God', in *The Church of Vatican II* ed. G. Barauna (London & New York, 1965); Y.-M. Congar 'The Church: the People of God' and R. Schnackenburg & J. Dupont 'The Church as the People of God', both in *Concilium* I, 1 (1965).

19. The new *Codex iuris canonici* heads its Book II 'De populo Dei', but in fact the canons dealing with the all the faithful in general are very few in number and vague in content.

20. See M.-D. Chenu *'Vox populi vox Dei.* L'opinione pubblica nell'ambito del popolo di Dio' in *La fine della Chiesa come società perfecta* (Milan, 1968) pp. 209–226; J.-M. Tillard, Le *Sensus fidelium.* Réflexion théologique' in *Foi populaire-Foi savante* (Paris 1976) pp. 9–40; also the articles by J.-L. d'Aragon, F. Dumont, E. R. Fairweather and E. Lamirande in the same volume.

Enrique Dussel

'Populus Dei' in Populo Pauperum: From Vatican II to Medellín and Puebla

THE QUESTION of the 'popular church' (*iglesia popular*) as a theological issue in need of clarification is immensely complex and cannot be given a quick explanation, as many critics have tried to do. I have to point out right from the beginning that part of the difficulty derives from the ambiguity, not just of the multi-faceted category 'people' (*pueblo*) but also of its various uses. 'People' may refer to the first people (Israel) or the new people (the Church); it may refer to the Gentiles (non-Christian) or a 'Christian people' (as in the Christian tradition of Latin America or Poland). John XXIII's expression 'the church *of the poor*', taken up in *Laborem Exercens* 8, may be an exact synonym of 'the popular church' if by 'popular' is meant the 'poor' of a Christian people. If, on the other hand, as we shall see, 'people' is taken as *gentes* (Gentiles), and it is said that 'The church is born *solely* of the people', the result is a sort of Pelagianism. Obviously to say, as has been said, that 'The church is born solely of the Holy Spirit,' is in turn a sort of monophytism.

On the other hand, if by 'church' are meant those Christians, part of the one official and institutional Church, who are being renewed, and evangelised, who make a choice for the poor, the oppressed and live among them, then this renewed 'church' (not a *new* church) can 'be born of the people' (from among the poor and oppressed, who in Latin America are already Christian, baptised and believers) through the action of the holy Spirit (which the theology of liberation has never denied). This is what is meant by Medellín, by Puebla, by the Christians who 'make the option' and live among the poor. It is absurd to say that the theology of liberation is the inspiration behind the popular church (in the sense indicated). The situation is precisely the opposite.

1. 'POPULUS DEI' AT VATICAN II (1962-1965)

If we take a historical perspective, no-one would have thought in 1965 that Chapter II of the constitution *De Ecclesia* would be the one we would be discussing, but Chapter III, on the bishops, which then appeared to be the central issue to put the definitions of Vatican I into their proper context.

The first schema 'De Ecclesia', presented on 1 December 1962, had a first chapter on 'the militant nature of the church' and a second on 'members of the church'.[1] Cardinal Liénart, in a speech which became famous, rejected the schema because only the juridical aspect was discussed (*mere iuridico appareat*),[2] and not the Church as mystery, the 'mystical' aspect (*in natura sua mystica*),[3] and ended with the ringing declaration, 'I love Plato, but I love truth more.' No less a person than Cardinal Koenig argued that the attribute of '*indefectibilitas fidei*' belonged to the 'believing people as a whole' (*populo credentium*),[4] since the faithful not only received doctrine, but also, 'as a community of believers' (*communitas fidelium*), had a positive influence on the *magisterium*. Mgr Devoto of Goya, Argentine, said that there was 'also a need for a clear and explicit restatement of the idea of the whole *people of God* . . . as the beginning of the whole constitution *De Ecclesia*.'[5] Cardinal Hengsbach too favoured the rejection of the schema for its 'clericalism and legalism' (*clericalismi et iuridismi*).[6] In the end the schema was rejected.

A theological commission worked to prepare the new schema, which was presented in Congregation 37 (30 November 1963). Fr Chenu tells how a Polish cardinal pressed for the doctrine of the 'societas perfecta', but the commission preferred the more biblical and spiritual idea of the 'people of God'.[7]

The question of the 'people of God' had already made its appearance in other conciliar schemas, as had that of the poor, the 'hungry multitudes'[8] who 'demand social justice'.[9] In the event, in the new schema 'The mystery of the Church'[10] was followed by the question of the episcopate and only in Chapter III that of 'The People of God and in particular about the laity'.[11] Immediately an important debate began. Does 'the people of God' mean the laity or the whole Church?. If it is the whole Church, it should come in Chapter II and the bishops in Chapter III. Cardinal Frings, for the Germans, proposed that Chapter II be devoted to the question 'Of the people of God'.[12] There was a change of meaning: from being only the laity, 'people of God' was transformed into a synonym for the Church. Some Latin Americans even then connected the issue of the 'people of God' with 'a greater apostolic dedication to the evangelisation *of the poor*'.[13]   In Congregation 54, on 23 October, Mgr Manuel Larraín spoke about the *Populus Dei*, emphasising its role of prophecy and martyrdom (witness), not 'passive acceptance', but active participation.[14]

Finally, in Congregation 80, on 15 November 1964, the 'corrected text' of Chapter II, 'De populo Dei', was presented.[15] With minor changes, this was to be the final text of *Lumen Gentium*. The opening statement, 'Christ is the light of all nations,' (LG 1), brings us right to the issue: *gentium* is not the same as *populorum*. But the terms used all refer to groups, communities, societies:

> It has pleased God, however, to make men holy and save them, not merely as individuals without any mutual bonds, but by making them into a single *people* . . . He therefore chose the race of Israel as a *people* unto himself. . . . [called together] the new *people* of God (LG 9).

This sets up a dialectic between a *first or old* people and a *new or second* people ('the *new* covenant').

A fundamental question, which will be central to the rest of this discussion, is the following: Does God call or summon individuals separately from their Gentile community or from the people of Israel, or does he call them communally? The Council is clear: he does not call them 'as individuals without any mutual bonds'. But, it could be objected, he forms the *new* people from the *old* people of Israel, but not from the Gentiles *as peoples*. It is true that the people of God is 'among all the nations of the earth' (LG 13), but there is no reference to 'Gentile peoples'. Nevertheless it would seem that we can say that the new people has been born from the old, from the 'remnant' of Israel (as Jesus was from Mary), by the work of the holy Spirit.[16] Jesus was part of the old people, Mary was, the apostles were. The *new* people was born by the holy Spirit of the old (the *flesh*): 'I will pour out my Spirit upon all flesh, and your sons and your daughters shall prophesy, and your young men shall see visions' (Acts 2:17). Israel is the flesh, as 'the Word became flesh' in Mary: it is the incarnation. Without *flesh* there would be no Christ; there would be only one nature (it would be monophytism). Without a *people* there would be no *new* people, but a collection of individuals 'without mutual bonds' (LG 9). Obviously the idea that the old people could have produced the new people by its own *potentia* (δυνάμει) is a negation of the incarnation of Christ, which is the fruit and the work of the holy Spirit himself; this is an absurd proposition which no Latin American theologian has even thought of putting forward.

Schema 1
The Origin of the Church

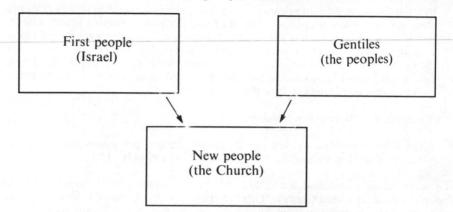

The important point is that, having *subsumed* in the holy Spirit, with Christ as head, by the will of the Father, the old people of Israel and the Gentiles ('Jew and Gentile, making them one, . . . to be the new people of God' LG 9), the *new* people, the Church, has been born, like Christ, in human history, into a specific people, into a *real* race, language and tradition, with *real* struggles and heroes. To take (on or up—*aufheben*) a historical people (Israel and the Gentiles) is to take the *flesh*, the history, the richness of the *previous* history of humanity. The history of peoples ('Israel according to the *flesh* wandered . . . in the desert,' of history, we may add) as communities, is 'made holy and saved' in the *new* people of God, and not just the ego-centred life of each individual who is called. It is a dialectic between the old 'people', and the new 'people', and not between an 'individual' (Christ) exclusively calling abstract 'individuals', without community, history, memories, struggles or martyrs.

At Vatican II the fact that the subject of the episcopate (Chap. III) was preceded by that of 'the people of God' *in genere* (Chap. II) was an explicit indication that the papacy, the episcopate, the ministerial priesthood, etc., are parts or elements *within* the 'people of God'.

2. THE 'PEOPLE OF GOD' AND 'POPULAR' PASTORAL WORK AT MEDELLÍN (1968)

At Medellín the double meaning of 'people' was taken over from Vatican II:

Just as Israel of old, the first People, felt the saving presence of God when he saved them from the oppression of Egypt, so we also, the new People of God, cannot but feel his saving passage (Introduction 6); . . . the hope that all the People of God, encouraged by the Holy Spirit, commit themselves to its complete fulfilment (i.e., of the work of the conference, *ibid.* end)

However, we immediately find a difference from Vatican II, not a contradiction, but added detail, elucidation, a Latin American touch:

> Among the *great mass* of the baptised in Latin America, the conditions of Christian faith, beliefs and practices . . . (6,I, 1, 'Pastoral Care of the Masses'). In evaluating popular religion, we cannot start from a Western cultural interpretation (6,I, 4). Faith, and therefore the Church too, is planted and grows in the different cultural forms taken by religion among different *peoples* (6,II, 5). 'Far from being satisfied with the idea that *the people* as a whole already possesses the faith, far from contenting herself with the task of preserving the faith of *the people* . . ., proposes . . . a serious re-evangelisation, . . . a reconversion . . . of our people, . . . which will push *the believing people* towards the twofold dimension of personal and community fulfilment . . . (since) according to God's will human beings are to be made holy and saved, not individually but as members of a community (6,II, 8–9).

And immediately afterwards we find:

> All manifestations of *popular* religion, such as pilgrimages, processions and devotional practices, should be imbued by the word of the Gospel (6,III, 12.).

These texts make it quite clear that by this time 'people' no longer has the same meaning as 'people of God' in *Lumen Gentium*. There are two reasons for this. The first is that 'the great mass of the baptised' in Latin America already form *a people*. 'People' means on the one hand the historical and cultural community and, on the other, the community of believers (the Church). In other words, in Latin America, because of the continent's amibiguous status as a 'Christian continent' (a Christian culture or civilisation), there is a confusion between 'people' in the sense of a social group in civil society and the 'people of God', the Church. On the other hand, even the people understood as a social group is not any longer a community of Gentiles, but, a 'Christian people'. This is why there can be a dialectic between a people already Christian but not sufficiently evangelised or converted and a people (Church) which is re-evangelised, re-converted. In this strict sense (the Christian people not sufficiently evangelised, the Christian people re-evangelised), we may find references to a *renewed, communitarian* 'Church', and so on.

These adjectives describe the church and groups within it, bishops, priets, religious, laity. They do not imply that those so described are a *different* church, one that is new, parallel, in opposition to the 'official' one, etc.

The second reason is that terms such as '*popular* religion' refer to the *real* poor, oppressed groups, classes ethnic groups, etc.: a social group consisting of the dominated. This is not the whole community, but a part:

> the material needs of those who are deprived of the minimum living conditions, and the moral needs of those who are mutilated by selfishness, . . . the oppressive structures that come from the abuse of ownership and power and from exploitation of workers or from unjust transactions (Introduction, 6).

'Popular' in this use means specific sectors of society, not the whole Christian people of Latin America. In this second sense the 'popular church' means that part of the 'people of God' (in the Vatican II sense) which is part of, or which has made a special commitment to re-evangelise, reconvert, the oppressed, the real poor, the exploited, the victims of repression and torture, etc. The adjective 'popular' comes to mean almost the same as what John XXIII meant by 'the church *of the poor*'—or at least one of its possible legitimate meanings:

'A deafening cry issues from millions of human beings, asking their pastors for a liberation which reaches them from nowhere else (14,I,2, 'Poverty of the Church'); In the context of poverty and even utter deprivation in which the majority of the Latin American people live, we bishops, priests.... (14,I,3). In this context a *poor* church denounces the unjust lack of this world's goods....' (14,II,5, italics added). With the help of all the people of God we hope to overcome the system of fees (14,III,13). For all the people of God they will be a continual call to evangelical poverty (14,III,16).

Of course, not everyone responds to these appeals for objective poverty, the poverty for which Francis of Assisi fought. Those who make a *real* response and commit themselves in their everyday lives to the *real* poor, the oppressed and exploited, are one part of the one institutional, official church. This part may be given the label 'popular church' because its members live among the real poor people, speak like them, suffer with them and fight for them: 're-evangelise', 'reconvert' (as Medellin says).

Some people, not without an express awareness of engaging in falsification, pronounce this church 'parallel', in opposition to the 'official' church, a 'different' church. Liberation theology has never sponsored these naive and simplistic terms, though that is not to say that a judge taking a phrase out of its context might not come across some expressions which might imply this deviant meaning.

Thus, on 6 May 1973, the bishops of the North-East of Brazil published a memorable document of the official, institutional Church, the one Church:

Confronted by the suffering of our people, their oppression and humiliation for so many centuries of our country's history, we have called on you [*convocar*, an ecclesial act *par excellence*] through the word of God to take up a position. We call on you to take up *a position alongside the people*, a position, more precisely, with all those who, *with the people*, commit themselves to work for their true liberation ... We are servants, ministers, of liberation .. . . As ministers of liberation, our first task is to be converted in order to serve better. We must accept this demand of the people of the North-East, who are crying out for this ministry of liberation, begging us to share their 'hunger and thirst for justice'.[17]

We could produce hundreds of other witnesses, but it is not necessary. The *popular* church (that is, those Christians who, as part of the one *official* church, make an effective commitment to the real poor) has been called 'the church born of the people'. This phrase provoked storms, mainly from those who had not opted for the real poor, the people of the oppressed and unjustly despoiled:

We are persecuted because we are *with the people*, defending their rights. The prelature of São Felix [said Mgr Casaldaliga] is a *persecuted church* because it has refused to be involved with the power of politics and money. And we shall be persecuted more and more because, by the power of God, we shall continue *at the side of the oppressed and poor*.[18]

Being with and among poor people is what it means to be a *popular* church. These people are a Christian people, and that is why the renewed, re-evangelised, reconverted church is born of the people, who are part of the same church (because they are the great believing, Christian mass of the baptised) through the holy Spirit of renewal of life. In no sense is this 'people' the 'Gentiles' of *Lumen Gentium*, and consequently there is no reason—as we shall shortly see—to fear a desire that the (non-Christian, Gentile) people may, exclusively from itself, produce the people of God, the Church.

Schema 2
The renewed (part of the) Church
which is born or proceeds from the Church as the (whole)
'Christian people'

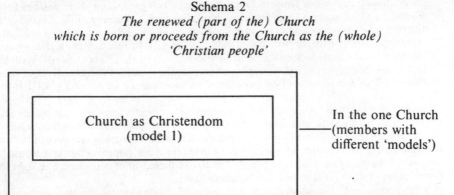

Church as Christendom
(model 1)

In the one Church
(members with
different 'models')

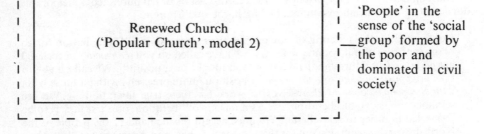

Renewed Church
('Popular Church', model 2)

'People' in the
sense of the 'social
group' formed by
the poor and
dominated in civil
society

3. 'PEOPLE OF GOD' AND 'BASIC ECCLESIAL COMMUNITIES' AT PUEBLA (1979)

The preparations for Puebla took place in an atmosphere of confusion, sometimes deliberately created. Take this commentary, for example:

> Without admitting the simplistic identification of the *people* (*pueblo*) with the *poor* (*el pobre*) and taking the expression People of God in the sense proposed by the Second Vatican Council . . ., it would be also perfectly correct to say that the People of God is the bearer of the Gospel, the subject of the Church. . . .[19]

Many levels are muddled here. 'People' (*pueblo*) in the first line is something like a sociological concept (like the 'social group' formed by the oppressed), and the author opposes its identification with the 'poor' (an identification which is, *sociologically*, quite possible, but has no theological implication one way or the other). It is obvious that to attempt to identify the sociological category 'people' with the 'people of God' of *Lumen Gentium* is an oversimplification which no theologian could make (not, that is, in the real meaning of a text, as opposed to a phrase taken out of context). But it can also be maintained that those who opt for or live in the situation of the people, among the real poor, as Christians ('the people of God' who make an option for the poor and share their lives, if we accept the phrase, which is not a tautology—the *popular* 'people of God'), are also, though not exclusively, bearers of the gospel and the subject of the Church. This sense—which is what those they attack intend and what their texts say—never occurs to the critics of the 'popular church', who are trying to find a *sect* in what is a legitimate *part* of the church, the one, official, institutional Church.

At Puebla the word 'people' was used in all the senses we have indicated, but there is often no clear realisation of the move from one sense to another. Let us look at some examples.

> CELAM created an environment among the Catholic *people* in which it could open itself with a degree of ease to a Church which also presented itself as a '*people*', (*pueblos*) a universal *People* which permeates other *peoples* (*pueblos*) (Puebla, 233). Our Latin American *people* (*pueblo*) spontaneously call a church 'God's house', . . . expressing the deepest and primary reality of the people of God (238)

It can be seen here that in *one case* the reference is to Latin American civil society, in *another* to society as a whole but as already Christian, and in other cases it is to the Church. It was in these not very well defined terms that the issue of the popular church was raised:

> The problem of the popular church, the church born of the people (*Iglesia popular, que nace del pueblo*) has several aspects. The first obstacle is surmounted if it is understood as a Church trying to become incarnate in the *popular* environments (*medios populares*) of our continent and so arising out of the response in faith of these groups to the Lord (263).

This sense, obviously, is the true meaning of the concept of the 'popular church', a part of the one Church, the people of God, which has made a commitment to the people in the sense of the *real* poor, oppressed, those who suffer, etc. In this sense the Church 'has been born' ('*Ecclesia orta sit . . .*' a council father said) *through* the work of the holy Spirit, *of* the flesh, *of* the historical people of Latin America, but as an Israel *already* chosen (because *already* in the Church, although its evangelisation has not finished): it has been 'reborn'. The popular church is the part of the Church (from cardinals, through bishops, priests, lay people, etc.) which has opted for or shares the lives of the *real* poor. It is not a 'parallel' church set against an 'official' Church. This Manichean excision is the product of a falsifying interpretation, which is still being put forward, but it is based on a wish to destroy the legitimacy of a legitimate part of the *one* Church.

At the same time there is an accusation of a sort of Pelagianism: the Church is born of the people (in the sense of the 'Gentiles'). From this we get to a contrary position, one which is certainly outside the conciliar tradition on the Church:

> This is the only way of being the church; *it is not born of the people*, but makes the people of God in that it is a call, . . . but it is not 'popular' in that it originates in the people as such.[20]

The attempt to deny legitimacy to a Pelagian position (the Church as 'people of God' is born totally of the people, in the sense of 'Gentiles') falls into a Monophysite position: the Church is born exclusively of God; no value is given to the flesh, the community which is called together. The call '*makes* the people'; in other words, each man or woman is made holy and saved 'individually and in isolation'—in contradiction of *Lumen Gentium*. There is no sense that the Church—as Puebla teaches in many texts—calls and takes to itself a 'people', a human 'community', and in so doing also enriches itself with all the historical fruits of those peoples. The 'people of God', the *new* people, is not born *solely* or *exclusively* either from the *first* people, nor solely of the Spirit, *excluding* the flesh. Without Mary there is no Christ, and equally without flesh there is no incarnation. Without a *people* which has been called there is no 'people of God'.

This, in any case, is not the issue in the discussion about the popular church, since it is not about the origin of the Church in the beginning (the *new* people, the Church, born of the *first* people, Israel, by the work of the holy Spirit and with Jesus as its head), but about the renewal, re-evangelisation, reconversion of an *existing* Church, one which is the Christian people but can still reach the full development of its faith. In other words, the '*renewed* church', which has been transformed by its option and by being poor with the poor, is born from the 'one, official Church', but it is born of the poor of that Church, of the oppressed people. This 'renewal' of the Church is born of the Christian people itself. There is, in addition, an organisational element, but not one in opposition to the official church, since it includes *part* of the whole official Church, from lay people and religious to bishops and cardinals:

> in a basic ecclesial community ... developing their union with Christ, they are searching for a more evangelical life in the midst of the *people* ...' 'The basic ecclesial communities are an expression of the Church's preferential love for the simple *people*' (Puebla, 641–643).

There can be no doubt that the basic ecclesial communities are, as it were, the natural habitat of Christians who belong to the oppressed people and the 'people of God', belong to the poor and belong to the Church. Not all the members of the Church opt for the poor or are poor. The basic community is also the appropriate place for the participation of the poor, the poor as a people, in the Church, the 'people of God', and for those who opt for them. The poor and those who opt for them, both being members of the 'people of God', can perfectly well be called the 'popular church'. *Church* is the noun, denoting the 'people of God' according to *Lumen Gentium*; *popular* is the adjective, implying a commitment to the poor and oppressed, the historical people, the social group consisting of the oppressed. In this sense, the 'popular church' means those Christians, *within the one official and institutional church*, who have a different 'model' (meaning vision and practice) of the type of evangelisation the Church should be carrying out in the world and among the poor, and so a different 'model' of the church to which they belong wholly and legitimately.

4. CONCLUSIONS

The 'popular church' or the Church committed to the poor, in solidarity with them, in the sense indicated, has been defined for us in general terms by John Paul II:

> The Church is passionately committed to this cause (of the workers) because she regards it as her mission, her service, as a proof of her fidelity to Christ, in order to be genuinely the Church of the poor. The poor are to be found in many forms: they appear in different places and at different times—in many cases we find them to be the product of the violation of the dignity of human work (*Laborem Exercens*, 8).

The Polish theologian Jozef Tischner, in his 'Ethics of Solidarity', has enabled us to see the importance to his local church of the concepts of 'country', 'nation' and 'freedom':

> The problem of the country faces us daily ... and arising from it is the question of the

preservation of the country. . . . This consciousness guides the whole nation. . . . Freedom is, as it were, a space in which we can move with security.[21]

In Latin America we have a different view of things. The 'people', rather than the country or the nation, is the chief protagonist of our current history, and this 'people' aspires, not so much to 'freedom' as to 'justice'. It is not a matter of being able to eat in freedom, but of having something to eat at all. Consequently, where some may talk of the '*national* church' or the church which embodies the *national* identity, in Latin America we feel that our 'identity' is embodied in a *popular* church. Devotion to Mary, for example, is 'popular': it was with the Virgin of Guadalupe on his banner that the priest Hidalgo fought against the Spanish in the nineteenth century to liberate Mexico, and the peasant Emiliano Zapato occupied Cuernavaca, also using as his banner a picture of our Lady of Guadalupe (taken from a church). And, 'as John Paul II has pointed out, [this devotion] is part of the innermost *identity* of these *peoples*' (Puebla, 283). 'Mary was also the voice which urged us to unity as human beings and Latin American *peoples*' (282).

There are people, even within the Church, with a clear desire to create confusion. In any situation, however, it is necessary to understand the experience of a particular church, such as that of Latin America, in order not to judge it simplistically in terms of different parameters, different cultures, nations or peoples. Our 'believing people' (*pueblo creyente*) deserves the respect of being listened to, of being incorporated into the 'people of God' as a historical people, with a memory, language and culture, with heroes, martyrs and saints. Archbishop Oscar Romero died for this 'people' with an *explicit* sense of being part of the '*popular* church'.

If someone asks us, for valid reasons, to give up a word, 'popular', it can go. But the underlying meaning was clearly stated by Pope John XXIII, and I may say that I had a deep personal experience of it with Paul Gauthier in Nazareth from 1959 to 1962, when we talked about 'Jesus, the Church and the poor' while working as carpenters in the Arab *shikum* in the village where Jesus said, 'The Spirit of the Lord has anointed me *to evangelise the poor*'. It is 'the church *of the poor*'.

Translated by Francis McDonagh

Notes

1. See *Acta Synodalia S. Conc. Oec. Vaticani Secundi*, I/1 (Vatican 1970); I/4 (Vatican 1971), Congregation 21.

2. *Ibid.* I/4, p. 127.

3. *Ibid.* p. 126.

4. *Ibid.* p. 133.

5. *Ibid.* p. 250.

6. Ibid. p. 254.

7. *Le Monde*, Paris (May 1983).

8. In Congregation 3, in the message to all human beings, the Council says, 'Caritas Christi urget nos . . . super turbam fame, miseria, ignorantia laborantem' (*Ibid.*, I/1, p. 225).

9. *Ibid.* p. 256. Mgr Enrique Rau remarked, referring to the 'language of the liturgy', that 'the Latin American view is that the mass is *for the people*, and how can they take part if they cannot understand?' (*Ibid.*, pp. 480ff).

10. *Ibid.* II/1, p. 216.

11. *Ibid.* pp. 256ff.

12. *Ibid.* p. 334.

13. *Ibid.* p. 798.

14. *Ibid.* II/2, pp. 236–26. Cardinal de Barros Camar also spoke on 'De Populo Dei in genere' (Congregation 51, 18 Oct. 1963, pp. 55ff.

15. *Ibid.* III/1 (1973) pp. 181ff.

16. 'The new Israel . . . is also called the church of Christ. For He has bought it for Himself with His blood, has filled it with His Spirit, and provided it with those means which befit it as a visble and social unity' (LG 9).

17. *SPES* (Lima) 4,21 (1973) 5ff; *Los obispos latinoamericanos entre Medellín y Puebla* (San Salvador 1978) pp. 40–63. See E. Dussel. *De Medellín a Puebla* (Mexico 1979) pp. 229ff.

18. See *Mensaje* (Santiago de Chile) 226 (1974) 52.

19. B. Kloppenburg *Informe sobre la Iglesia popular* (Mexico 1978) p. 58.

20. J. Lozano Barrangan *La Iglesia del Pueblo* (Mexico 1983) p. 106.

21. Italian translation, Bologna 1981, p. 137.

PART II

Redefining Ecclesial Roles from within the Experience of the Church with the Poor

Alois Lorscheider

The Re-defined Role of the Bishop in a Poor, Religious People (*Meio Popular Pobre e Religioso*)

THE PURPOSE of this contribution is to provide a narrative account of the process of finding one's way, how this is learnt and taught, how the people can see their own faith confirmed by that of the bishop, and how the bishop can strengthen his faith through the faith of the people.

I was consecrated bishop on 20 May 1962, taking charge of the diocese of Santo Angelo, in Rio Grande do Sul, Brazil, on 12 June of that year. In 1973 I was transferred to the North-East of Brazil, to the diocese of Fortaleza, in the State of Ceará.

Soon after coming to Fortaleza, in August 1962, I began to experience a change in how I saw the episcopal ministry. In the south, it seemed to me, I had been far more the person who teaches what he knows, without any great concern for the problems specifically affecting the poor. It was a simple transmission of a store of knowledge, leaving the people to decide how it could be applied to their lives.

My sacramental celebration followed much the same lines as my doctrinal approach. It was a celebration of the mystery of faith all right, but without paying much attention to the aspect of its meaning in the lives of the people. The existing ecclesial communities had their origin more in worship than in a quest for solutions to real problems in the light of faith. The liturgy was largely a celebration of the Word since there were not enough priests to provide for eucharistic celebration in most of the area.

I carried the faith to the people like a ready-made story, without reflecting much on its meaning in the socio-political-economic-cultural sphere in which those people lived. I was more of a teacher and president of the liturgy than a real evangeliser within the actual experience of the people.

In Fortaleza, in contact with another type of basic ecclesial community, springing in the first place not from the need to worship, but from one to find Christian solutions to the specific problems facing the people in their lives, my episcopal ministry, in its triple function of teaching, sanctifying and governing, began to take on a different aspect.

A first approach that influenced this change was that I began to listen to the people. The fact of being new to the region, ignorant of its history and culture and sometimes even finding its language difficult, meant that I had to listen in order to find out what was really going on. Starting with a need at first, this listening soon became something more. It became a habit, a discovery that led to a complete change in me and my ministry.

The people were slow in their speech, and even more so in their thought, but very specific in the way they applied the Word of God to their experience of life in a deeply evangelising way. They were communicating not knowledge, but *experience*, a *way of life* that could be glimpsed, a life of faith with deep roots in reality. And not just this: I observed a brotherly frankness in which the most delicate problems could be dealt with in the community in an atmosphere of considerable calm, drawing conclusions of the utmost practicality.

For example, in one community, a young man had behaved improperly to a girl during a dance. The case was dealt with at a community meeting, held at night, with the young people concerned present, and their parents, together with other members of the community, including children. With the greatest naturalness, very slowly, the case was approached, discussed, and finally resolved. For me, that night was a great experience.

I have been present at numerous other similar occasions, always with the same result. For me, this is taking part in the finest examples of fraternal correction I have ever known in my life. The most interesting aspect of them is the community's determination that such things should not happen again. And my role as bishop? I did nothing except be present and listen. They did not ask my opinion nor did I think it right to intervene. They themselves, as a community, brought the process to its necessary conclusion. My presence did not even cause them any embarrassment. It was as if they were carrying on with the normal pattern of community life. And sometimes this was the first occasion I had visited a particular community . . .

In a short while it became clear to me that my episcopal ministry would be exercised in a different way. I would always be an extra member of a community, with my own special responsibility in it, but without seeing myself or being seen as the head of that community, as superior to it; rather, as a member of the community vested with Christ's *exousia* for the sacrament of order, I should be there only to serve at the moment when they felt a need for the service I could give, or when I felt, in the spirit of fraternal charity, that I could be a help to them on their way. I was no longer the teacher or instructor, but one animator among a lot of other animators. I too had to become a pupil before thinking of being a master. But I no longer see myself as master, because there is only one Master. I think of myself far more as being a disciple, with them, of the Master, listening to Jesus and his Spirit, attentive with the whole community to what Jesus and the Spirit have to say to the Church.

In this way, the eucharistic celebration itself, and the celebration of the other sacraments began, within my life as bishop, to take on another dimension: celebrating, with the community, the mystery of faith by inserting it as far as possible into the context of the lives of the members of the community, so that it was also a celebration of their lives. The liturgy itself began to take a different shape.

To take the allegory of the Good Shepherd (John 10) as an illustration, I no longer saw myself as someone leading my flock, but as someone walking in the middle of the flock, together with the flock, without for a moment hiding the figure of the one true shepherd, Jesus Christ.

In this context of the communities made up of poor, religious people (*meio popular pobre e religioso*), I made another discovery: a new way of praying.

The people begin each and every meeting with a reading from the Word of God. This Word is then interiorised for a few moments, in silence; next there comes a very lively exchange of what the Word of God suggests to each participant in the context of their own lives, often ending with a formal spontaneous prayer. The most noteworthy aspect of this beginning every meeting with the Word of God is that it seems to leave its mark on the whole day, turning the whole meeting into a great prayer that receives its crown in the evening with the celebration of the Eucharist.

I see in this a happy harmony between faith and life, between action and prayer.

The way the poor, religious people of the communities regard their bishop is something that never fails to make an impression on me. How they desire the presence of the bishop! The bishop's presence at their meetings, in their daily lives, is what they appreciate most. They see it as an enormous support, a stimulus that leaves them happy, full of courage and enthusiasm. The bishop can spend the whole day at one of their meetings without opening his mouth; his presence alone is everything to them. Nevertheless, it does sometimes happen that they openly ask the bishop for his opinion, and he does have perfect freedom to intervene when he thinks it convenient or necessary.

For me, pastoral visitations have become far easier to carry out. I no longer need to prepare lists or catechisms. Everything springs from the lives of these poor and deeply religious people. Their feeling for faith is a reality one can touch with one's hands.

Today I also see the problem of vocations in the Church in a different light. The real problem is how to gather people together in small, living, apostolic communities, not how to herd them into seminaries and convents. The small ecclesial communities will produce the various ministries and services the People of God need. There is a whole new structure of ecclesial experience coming to life. The problem now is how to form these ministers and servers in the spirit of Christ and his Church.

Finally, this new way of being a bishop based on very concrete contact with the communities of the poor and religious people leads the bishop to a simpler life-style, making him feel the need to identify himself more and more with the Poor Christ and the poor people (*os pobres*), avoiding anything that can give an impression of greatness or ruling status. The bishop becomes a brother among brothers.

These, then, are some aspects of the life of the communities that have taught me how to be a bishop today in the Third World—and perhaps also in the First.

Translated by Paul Burns

John Mutiso-Mbinda

The Presbyter

1. INTRODUCTION

MY TESTIMONY has to be seen within a particular context in a Third World, in Africa and in Kenya where I have exercised my presbyteral ministry in the last fifteen years. I am very much aware of my own social/cultural situation in which I was born, socialised, grew and was educated in a foreign system of education which has led me into a cultural alienation. I am also aware of my historical context in which I was born, grew up in the midst of exploitation of human beings by a foreign government and the struggle of my people that led to liberation in 1963. The same year I decided to go for my seminary formation. I was fortunate to follow the developments and results of Vatican II 1962—1965.

Politically my country became independent but remained economically too dependent on foreign mechanisms and systems of domination. My country in which I practise my priestly life is a divided country. There are two groups of people: The owners and the workers. Due to higher wages offered to technical workers, professionals and executives, a new middle class is gradually emerging. The movement to urban and town centres has brought in a new phenomenon of growing marginals who are landless, unemployed or destitute. In the rural village level there is still a strong sense of community which forms a strong base for the new image of the Church—the popular church, a church of the poor where they are actually rich in the way they celebrate their faith using the rich symbols, artform and expressions from their own culture.

2. TESTIMONY

My testimony emerges from this context in which I feel I have grown tremendously as a result of being challenged in my style of priestly ministry and in my attitude to the people to whom I minister. It has been a slow but painful growth.

Soon after my ordination in 1968, I took my assignment in a rural parish where I was supposed to learn from my experienced parish priest but after one month he left for Ireland on home leave. I was to be the acting parish priest for almost five months. I had no choice but to continue with the system I inherited by organising everything from the top of a pyramid. My role for the next five months was mainly sacramental or cultic and since not much emphasis had been placed on the importance of meaningful liturgical celebration, even this role was not so well played. I was too busy trying to organise the parish that my contact with the people was indirect and sporadic. I went around the parish outstations saying masses, sometimes five on a Sunday! Consequently I did not get to know the people and I had a feeling of the lack of community. My style was simply too mechanical. I did not know any better for this is what I had learnt in the seminary. I was dealing with large numbers of people and the quality did not matter very much as long as you had many baptisms, confessions, holy communions and large crowds. I was wondering why so few people were involved in parish activities despite the fact that they were so many. I was the centre of all parish life and activities, leading in all the celebrations. At Mass I often times led the whole liturgy of the Word while people listened; I also led the singing since I felt I was an expert and that people might make a mess of it or not know when to sing. I assumed a lot of ignorance on the part of the laity—after all, I had done my philosophy and theology! By the end of my five month experience as parish priest I became an 'expert' in one model of the Church—the pyramidical model in which I was the boss and knew the answers to almost every question. My catechists learnt the same style of ministry and they too were small 'parish priests' in their outstation. I had very little time if any for on-going study and reading and consequently became almost alienated from the changes that were taking place during the early post-Vatican period. I was not aware of any post-conciliar documents until I took four years of study leave.

Since then I began to become aware of the discrepancies that existed between my priestly ministry and the context in which I was exercising it. Upon completion of my studies in sociology I was appointed to another rural parish and despite my studies I did not know where to start but one thing was sure—I was determined to go where the people were and to take their life situation seriously. With the help of the catechist we carried out a parish survey in order to get some basic facts about the parish situation. Out of this survey I discovered that there are 100,000 people in the parish of which 60% were youth 20% Catholic, and only 15% of the total population could read and write. 95% of the people were engaged in subsistence farming and cattle rearing with the remaining 5% working in cities and towns.

One major need that emerged very clearly from this parish survey was one for leadership training. As a result a leadership workshop was organised at which three people from each Mass centre were present. This initial workshop was so successful that it triggered off a whole programme for parish renewal and initiated attitude changes concerning the parish structure and the role of the priest in this renewed model of the parish.

The growth towards base communities at village level started at a follow-up workshop on how to use the Bible at a prayer meeting or worship services in the absence of the priest. Spontaneously village base communities of prayer and Bible reflection started near the parish and I was invited to pray with each community in turn. I had to make a choice in order to strengthen these base village neighbourhood communities that were now becoming communities of living faith, prayer and reflection. Soon I begun to realise why these base communities were becoming so well established. They are natural groupings at village or neighbourhood level where people know each other and meet informally face to face.

Because of a natural sense of community, the people at each base community respond spontaneously to cases of human need, misfortunes such as sickness or death. Soon this became a faith response overflowing from the base community prayer life. A genuine solidarity can be seen at community events such as marriages, births, funerals and particularly in the sharing of expenses for these events and contributing physically to the preparation of feasts for the occasions. Gradually, a new way of being Church was emerging at this base village community level—a church with a human face. These base

Christian communities were gradually becoming self-ministering as they met in one another's homes weekly 'persevering in prayer and praising God'.[1] This new development raised many questions in my mind regarding my role as an ordained minister in a based Christian community. I soon began to realise that this was the image of the church described by Vatican II in reference to the common priesthood of the faithful and the ministerial priesthood in which we all, each in its proper way, share in the one priesthood of Christ.[2] In accepting this new model of Church and the renewed image of the presbyter, I was greatly influenced by the final message of the Bishops of AMECEA at their Plenary of 1973 who stated among other things: 'We are convinced that in these countries of Eastern Africa it is time for the Church to become truly 'local' that is self-ministering, self propagating and self-supporting. Our planning is aimed at such local churches for the coming years. We believe that in order to achieve this, we have to insist on building Church life and work on basic Christian communities, in both rural and urban areas.[3] Another statement that helped me in clarifying the renewed role of the presbyter comes from the conclusions of the AMECEA Plenary of 1976: 'The Christian communities we are trying to build are simply the most local incarnations of the one, holy, Catholic and apostolic Church. The Church of Christ is truly present in all legitimate local congregations of the faithful, which, united with their pastors, are themselves called "Churches" in the New Testament. . . .'[4]

I have become more convinced that this ecclesiology of base Christian communities is the renewed ecclesiology of Vatican II in which I must find the meaning of my presbyteral ministry. In this ecclesiology of communion as outlined in *Lumen Gentium* and *Presbyterorum Ordinis*,[5] I have come to see ministry as within the base community rather than above it. I have become a true 'discipulus', a learner in the community and not a person who knows the answers to all the questions. Together we search for the meaning of our present life—our story in the light of the Gospel—God's story. It has dawned on me that I have actually in the past been overplaying my role of presbyter to the extent that I deprived very gifted people in the base community from contributing to the life and growth of the community. In order to overcome this problem I have prepared a team of able lay men and women to work closely with me in specific ministries that have emerged from the base Christian communities.[6] Together we have spent much time in training community prayer leaders who can guide Bible reflection sessions and prayer events of the communities; family and marriage counsellors to guide and help married couples, before, during and after marriage; mediators or promoters of community spirit, who help to mediate and help to effect reconciliation whenever there are disputes or conflicts in the community; we have a base level development co-ordinator to help promote education for awareness and the implementation of community projects. We have an overall co-ordinator of each base community who continually guides the carrying out of the various ministries in the community. Although I continue to be an indispensable co-ordinator of the whole parish, my ministry has become more adapted to this new model of the Church, the popular church. I continue to carry out my specific priestly role liturgical and sacramental ministry and taking my responsibility of training efficient over-all co-ordinators at base community level. One of my vital functions is to continue to be the living link between the base Christian communities and the parish as a whole, between the parish community and my Bishop and through him with the universal Church.

The proclamation of the Word has become a delightful responsibility since now I proclaim it to a people whose life situation and story I have come to know, love and appreciate. They continue to evangelise me as I proclaim God's Word. I have come to realise the importance of listening and my own poverty in this regard. I must now learn as a faithful 'discipulus' to listen in prayerful reflection at the feet of my only Teacher—Christ, so that I may proclaim his message to others. It has not been easy learning to listen to my team members and having to receive feedback from them. I am continually reminded to have an openness to the various gifts of the spirit in the community. In humble service, I must accept to be a brother among brothers although I am called 'father' and 'teacher'.[7]

Arising from this renewed image and role of the presbyter my people's expectation is that I become more of a facilitator than a solitary ruler, more of a listener than a speaker, more of a mediator than one who takes sides. The people themselves have come to teach me that leadership and authority is not a question of sitting on a chair and telling people what to do or what not to do, but in evangelical terms it is a service modelled on Christ the servant, who washed the feet of disciples to show them what authentic authority means. I have come to learn that the poor people at base community level have nothing to administer and therefore the emphasis is not so much on administration but on building human relations. Efficiency, results, and time factor are not a priority but what matters most is the process of humanisation, the life of the base community. I have often found myself very impatient with this clumsy way of approach to life but I had to die to self and be one of the people. Both administration and human relations are important but I realised I had been educated to over-emphasize administration. I am now convinced that a very important role of the presbyter is that of mediation, reconciliation and bringing about healing in a base Christian community. My role has often been one of 'bridge-building' between individuals, families, neighbourhoods, villages, clans and tribes. At times we find ourselves in difficult issues when we talk till we agree. If there is no agreement or consensus today, tomorrow is another day! Dialogue plays an important part in my ministry and with it the ability to listen with the heart. In the process of dialogue, discussion and prayerful reflection at base community level. I have witnessed healing gradually take shape giving the sacrament of reconciliation a deeper meaning.[8]

3. CONCLUSION

A number of conclusions emerge from my testimony and I thought these may serve as a conclusion to my present view of the renewed role of the presbyter.

(a) No dichotomy

Because of the total integrated world-view and approach to life of the poor at base Christian community, I have been led to a realisation that there is no dichotomy between life and faith, theory and practice, development and pastoral work. Holiness for my people is not some abstraction that touches only the soul, the spiritual, but is an integral wholeness that touches the body, the matter, the world. A Tswana elder asked by David Livingstone what holiness (*boitsepho* in Tswana) was had the following to say: 'When copious showers have descended during the night, and all the earth and leaves and cattle are washed clean, and the sun rising shows a drop of dew on every blade of grass, and the air smells fresh—that is holiness.'[9] Notice that there are no abstract terms in this description. Authentic holiness and spirituality must be integral. This has been my experience at base Christian community level when on New Year's Day we had a Eucharistic celebration at which cattle, seeds, tools, chickens, and any symbols of work were blessed.

(b) Breaking in of the Kingdom

Gradually, I witnessed the breaking of the kingdom at base Christian community as many of the barriers that divide human beings are slowly being removed through the education for awareness programme. The marginals of society, (the despised one, the forgotten ones, people with disability of all sorts), are slowly brought to the centre, the oppressed (through ignorance and lack of awareness) are set free, the powerless are gradually regaining control of their own lives and destiny, the voiceless (rendered so by the mass approach and an over-emphasis on administration rather than human relations) are beginning to speak for themselves, the uprooted ones are once more rooted in their own culture through a process of inculturation at various levels, the absent ones are now returning from 'exile' as they find more meaning of life at base Christian community level and the formerly non-invited are beginning to feast at the Eucharistic banquet. Each base community is consciously involved in the agenda of the coming of the Kingdom in a very practical way. My belief that creation is not a finished product has enable me to lead the people to the decisive task of a 'World to be build up and brought to fulfilment' to borrow a phrase from *Gaudium et Spes* No. 93.

(c) Planning

I have come to realise that this agenda of the Kingdom is too important to be left to chance and haphazard happening. I have come to appreciate planning as a conciliar process whereby the base Christian community, which is a communion of communions in the parish, is actively involved and participating in shaping its own future. Through interchange and complementarity of gifts and charisms we have often times diserned together the signs of the times. We have had an experience of the Body of Christ where all the members have a part to play. We have discovered that this can only happen in the context of a listening base community. I have come to realise that planning is one way in which we take seriously our God-given role as makers of history, as co-creators with him. 'Praxis', or social action to transform the world and society, to me means that our faith be a commitment to specific actions, to definite programme—to planning. This for me is an ecclesial and corporate action.

(d) Metanoia

Conversion of heart, mind, and attitudes to see people in the world and approach to life as Christ sees it is at the very heart of the renewed role of the presbyter. This has led me to an openness to a new approach to others. It is a violent and slow process of death to self involving self-emptying and giving up my own prejudices and pre-conceptions. It has been very painful to be truly attentive to others and to what they see as important for them. The greater part of my conversion has been as a result of being evangelised by the poor people at base community level in their struggle for survival, as they suffer one misfortune after another and yet maintaining a deep faith in a God who saves those who believe in him and in his Son Jesus the risen Lord. I have to make this basic spirituality of 'Kenosis' part of my life as a priest leading me to accept shared leadership, team work and mutual responsibility as part and parcel of the renewed pastoral approach of the presbyter.

(e) People-oriented ministry

Part of my conversion has been to change from a task-oriented style of ministry to a people-oriented style, a ministry as though people, and not things, matter most. In my own seminary formation the emphasis was on the administration of things, institutions etc. Now I must learn to place more emphasis on the people and not things, on human relations and not administrations, on the humanising process and not results. Both orientations are necessary and therefore the major problem is adjusting in such a way that there is a balance. The times when I strike this balance it has become quite clear to me that people are not objects but subjects of evangelisation.

Notes

1. Acts 2:42–47

2. Vatican II, *Lumen Gentium*, No. 10 where this image is described clearly with the relevant distinctions. See also *Presbyterium Ordinis*, No. 2 which brings up the same image.

3. *AFER*, Vol. XVI No. 1 and 2, pp. 9–10

4. *AFER*, Vol. 18, No. 5, p. 250. Here the Bishops make reference to *Presbyterorum Ordinis* Nos. 2, 6

5. Vatican II

6. This diversification of Ministries is very much emphasised by Pope Paul VI, *Evangelii Nuntiandi*, No. 73, where he stresses training as essential.

7. *Presbyterorum Ordinis*, No. 9

8. *Ibid.*

9. Livingstone, D. *Expedition to the Zambesi*, p. 64.

Religious Life Among the Poor: Two accounts from Brazil

FROM 13 to 15 August 1981, in Lagoa Seca, in the state of Paraíba, Brazil, there was a meeting of about 320 men and women religious from small communities living among the poor. They met to exchange experiences and deepen religious life in this type of involvement. The texts of the accounts and the reflections stimulated by the reports have been collected in a book published in Recife, Pernambuco, Brazil, under the title *Caminhada das pequenas comunidades da vida religiosa inserida* ('The Journey of the Little Communities of the Inserted Religious Life'). From 16 to 19 August 1984 another meeting was held to study the importance of popular religion (*religisidade popular*) in revitalising the experience of God in religious life. Here we present two accounts from the 1981 meeting, which sketch, in simple terms, the new shape of religious life in poor and working-class environments.

1. THE SMALL COMMUNITIES OF NATAL (RIO GRANDE DO NORTE), 1964–1982

On 25 February 1964 a community of sisters of the Congregation of the Immaculate Heart of Mary took up residence in the city of Taipu, Rio Grande do Norte, to attempt basic ecclesial work. After receiving information and advice from the Apostolic Administrator and Vicar General, the four sisters, Sr Natalina Maria Rossetti, Sr Theresa Piovesan, Sr Terezinha Mazzurana and Sr Luiza Fagundes, aware of their mission, embarked on their pastoral activities. To help them in attaining their objectives they had adopted the following guidelines:

– to seek to understand the local situation by means of a socio-economic, cultural and religious survey;
– to make contact with the members of the community through coordinated pastoral work, based on reflection;
– to seek to promote personal development among members of the community through genuine friendship and by showing them how they could serve their fellows;
– to educate the community about the aims and objectives of parish work by showing them that they had come to work with them, to make the same journey;
– to study and reflect continually on their pastoral work in accordance with the diocesan pastoral plan.

The first step was a Better World Movement course, to create greater awareness of Christian life and greater commitment.

At first the sisters regarded themselves as present in the parish community to solve the

56

problem of the shortage of priests, but gradually they became aware that they had a role of their own, one which was specific to their vocation. They came to see that the religious life is based on the consecration conferred by baptism, and that it should seek to enter more and more fully into the lives of the people.

In the beginning the sisters were in a great hurry and wanted to do a lot in a short time, but as they thought more about their work they realised that *it is necessary to respect the pace and the different stages of the people's slow journey* and to integrate oneself totally into that process.

After drawing up a plan of work, the sisters realised that its success would depend on study, reflection, prayer and regular review. This led them into a new way of life in fraternity. As a result the union in charity and action which existed among the team was given visible form in a commitment to the evangelical counsels, a commitment presented to those outside as a sign to bring them to carry out their Christian duties. They came to the conclusion that pastoral work at the base is possible only when it is the fruit of a genuinely fraternal life, like the communal life of the first Christians. At the very beginning it was not easy to live this 'inserted' religious life with integrity and balance because of differences in ways of life, customs and culture, because the sisters who had come to the north for this work were from the south of Brazil. It required a constant effort to give this community life appropriate expression.

Living 'inserted' into the ecclesial community, the sisters discovered the real meaning of poverty, complete availability for the service of one's neighbour, the courage to take an active part in the Church's journey and to renew oneself, abandoning everything that no longer has any meaning for the religious life. Today we would say 'making an option for the poor'. What made the deepest impression on the people was the visits the sisters made to their poor houses, in friendship, and a desire to help them, their assistance on various occasions, a death, family problems, and so on. They encouraged people, took part in their celebrations and talked to everyone, helping them to discover their values and their Christian mission. The people were moved by the charity which had made the sisters leave their families, possessions and land in the south to come and live with them.

In all this the sisters found meaning in living the evangelical counsels, in a journey of commitment and presence 'inserted' among their less privileged brothers and sisters, God's chosen, and were glad to be able to serve the church in Natal.

When the need arose for a greater Church presence in the rural areas and the small towns of the interior of Rio Grande do Norte, some religious went to live more directly among the poor. As a result new small communites have grown up in various parts of the diocese which the bishops indicated as the most deprived. At present we have 47 sisters from eight congregations working in 20 small communities, 20 of them in small towns and in the rural areas. Then in 1981 another was established on the outskirts of Natal. Later the small communities undertook responsibility for planning, reflection and holding meetings in order to work together to come closer to the people. With hope and courage, we are beginning to reorganise and plan our future meetings. With the help of an ecclesiastical adviser, we are studying subjects such as political education, popular religion, presence among the people, reviews of progress and forward planning. The meetings take place every two days and each group has ideas and experience to contribute from its work. The small communities are showing great interest in this form of presence among the people, and enjoy the complete support of the local bishops, who have already shown solidarity in difficult moments in the lives of some rural communities which experienced tensions as a result of stands they had taken in support of the people when they had been unjustly treated by some local authorities. This has given us courage to continue our work of liberating evangelisation. We are also very grateful to have at our meetings the advice of an ecclesiastical assistant to indicate the way ahead for us in our continuing journey alongside the people of God.

2. THE SMALL COMMUNITIES OF PARAÍBA 1969–1982

(a) The beginning

The small religious communities grew out of a double search. The first was the wish of the local church to find a new direction for religious life, to bring it closer to the people and enable it to be of real service to them. The second was the sisters' own search, in response to challenges from various quarters, the challenge to follow Jesus and the Gospel more radically, the challenge of their own situation, the sufferings of the people and their thirst for liberation, the demands of the Church after the Second Vatican Council and Medellín, and their feeling of the need to renew the structures of religious life.

The group formed by the small communities of Paraíba, in the Brazilian North-East, is now in its fourteenth year of existence. The first community was set up in Pitimbu in 1969 and was later followed by others. Some chose to work in the rural areas, others in the towns, where they established themselves in the outskirts. At present the group has 22 communities, making a total of about 65 people. The members belong to 13 different religious congregations. In the rural areas there are eight small communities; the other 14 are in the outskirts of the cities and in the towns of the interior. Eight small communities in the Brejo area are making this journey with us, but since December 1981 they have been part of the new diocese of Guarabira. These eight communities have members from four different congregations. There are thus 30 small communities in all.

(b) Development and organisation

The first stage, in the early years, was dominated by our effort to have a presence in solidarity and friendship with the people, and by our gradual discovery of the local situation. While we never abandoned this work, which is fundamental, as our journey continued our range of activity expanded, and gradually identified with the emergence and maturing of communities and small groups among the people as they gradually organised. As the sisters gained more experience, a greater internal organisation of the communities became necessary. The system of organisation is flexible, and corresponds to the natural rhythms of our lives. It is maintained by a sharing of friendship and an exchange of experience among communities (through visits, contact and solidarity at significant moments), meetings twice a year, an annual retreat, and a coordinating group consisting of a team of sisters who serve for three years.

The meetings are prepared in relation to the concerns of the moment. The issues are those which the needs of the mission confront us with, and these issues have marked, and still mark, our journey. For example, in 1971 we discussed the aims of our mission, difficulties encountered, aspects of continuity, religious life and insertion and commitment in our surroundings, conscientisation among ourselves and in the local community. In 1972 we studied 'The Unity between Presence to God and Presence to People', in 1973 'Our Commitment in the Brazilian Situation', in 1974 'Relationships in our Work, in our Everyday Lives, in Accepting Others in Community'. In 1975 the themes were 'Trade Unions and Liberation Theology'. In 1976 a review of our attitudes to liberation in practice, 'Signs of Oppression and Signs of Liberation', 'An Overall View of the Capitalist System and Education for Liberation'. In 1977 'Popular Religion and the Mission of Liberation in the Light of the Word of God', in 1978 'The Church Emerging from the People', 'Small Communities, Professional Work and Mission'. 1979 was devoted to 'A Review of the Ten Years of the Journey of the Small Communities of Paraíba'. Themes from 1980–1981 were 'Small Communities and Re-reading the Bible', 'The Approach of the Small Communities in the Present Situation of Latin America' and 'The Role of Popular Groups in Genuine Democratic Politics'. In 1982, which was the year of elections for the governor, deputies, prefects and councillors, the theme was 'Political Parties and Popular Vocations'.

The small communities have a common fund which helps to finance the meetings and retreats and meets the most urgent needs of the sisters of the religious communities.

(c) Criteria for new small communities

When new small communities want to come to the archdiocese, they have to consult, in addition to the bishop, the coordinating committee of the small communities and the area leaders about where they should live. The small communities have to observe the pastoral guidelines of the archdiocese. On first coming to the archdiocese, new sisters of the small communities have to spend a preparatory period of a few months in other small communities.

(d) Difficulties and challenges

– The socio-political and economic system of Brazil, in which the mass of the people are enslaved and are sometimes not even aware of their oppression;
– the results of our past, which was generally devoted to educating the bourgeois middle class;
– the habit of giving orders, teaching and leading;
– unpreparedness for a life of risks and social conflicts;
– impatience in mission and difficulty in accepting and respecting the pace of the people;
– unpreparedness for community life;
– sometimes a lack of judgment on the part of the congregations in the selection and sending of sisters;
– tension between work as a means of earning a living and closer contact with the poor and the demands of pastoral activities.

(e) What we have gained

– Religious life in the small communities is gradually regaining its character of prophecy and service;
– openness to the world, to the historical and socio-political dimension, in our religious commitment;
– an increasing discovery of the presence of God in the world, in the events in the lives of the poor (incarnation, committed contemplation);
– greater unity between faith and life;
– the experience of the blessings of opposition and marginalisation when we commit ourselves to the cause of the poor;
–a strengthening of hope in a Church growing out of the people through the spirit of God;
– a realisation that we too are evangelised by the poor;
– a dismantling of our models of security;
– an experience of a life of fraternity and sharing (in the community and with the people);
– growth in a prayer life which celebrates life, in a religious outlook which more closely accompanies God's plan;
– growth in a feeling and practice of community with the local church;
– a realisation that we cannot be self-sufficient, that we need to find new expressions of our service of the kingdom of God;

– clearer realisation of the need for a constant review of our lives and a modification of our plans, attitudes and actions;

– an ever greater conviction that the power to transform the world and society comes from the lowly.

A crucial factor has been the practical support of the local church and its bishop, Dom José Maria Pires, who continues to give us, as he has always done, an area of freedom in which we feel trusted. We are journeying with our church in communion in the option for the poor and its consequences.

From the beginning we have also had the invaluable help of Fr René Guerre, who is still our friend and adviser, and of many brothers and sisters, theologians, religious, men and women, and lay people, who have helped us in our reflection and, sometimes, with fruitful questions.

Translated by Francis McDonagh

Gustavo Gutiérrez

The Task of Theology and Ecclesial Experience

I HAVE been asked for a personal statement about the task of theology in relation to the basic ecclesial communities. As I am offering my personal experience, I shall speak, at least partly, in the first person. This makes it a more difficult undertaking than a purely abstract treatment of the subject would be. It is also difficult because I am uncertain where to begin. I will try one approach, well aware that there are others.

(a) During my years as a university student and as a member of lay apostolic groups, I, like my friends, was anxious to acquire a fuller and better knowledge of Christian doctrine. This was what we called the aspect of study or formation, which we saw as a necessary condition for action, in accordance with the famous principle expressed in the demanding formula: 'No one can give what they do not have.' This study consisted in obligatory but brief biblical commentary; the analysis of encyclicals, both about social matters (*Rerum Novarum, Quadragesimo Anno*) and more strictly doctrinal ones (*Mediator Dei, Mystici Corporis*) and some occasional —often unfinished—reading of authors such as R. Guardini, K. Adam etc.

In those days the term 'theology' was unfamiliar to us and we thought of it as existing on some high unattainable plane. According to a well known priest, perhaps we always associated theology with German names and the German language, which only increased our feeling of the distance between us and what we considered a matter for specialists.

Later, as a first year theology student trying to assimilate Peruvian and Latin American literature and experience, one subject interested me above all: the introduction to theology. The question of the meaning and function of our understanding of the faith in Christian and ecclesial life, seemed to me not only to come before any other question but also to be *the* central and decisive question, as well as always remaining an open one. I was passionately devoted to the study of the first question in St Thomas Aquinas' *Summa Theologica*, Melchor Cano's contribution to the places for theology (*loci theologici*) and the classic book by Gardeil on these issues. Over several vacations I devoured the article 'Theology' by Y. Congar (in the *Dictionary of Catholic Theology*). His historical perspective got me out of an almost exclusively rational way of looking at theological work. It opened my mind to other ways of seeing (that of the Tübingen School, for example). My discreet reading of the book by M. D. Chenu *The Saulchoir School* revealed the whole scope of human history to me and the life of the Church itself as a place for theology.

One result of this interest was that in the theological treatises I read afterwards I paid close attention to the methodological aspect and to the relation between theology and the sources of revelation. Many of my professors helped in this by their insistence on the Bible.

As a student, one of the things I tried to do was to deepen my own knowledge, so that later I could teach this aspect of theology, as it seemed to me a useful way of situating theology's why and wherefore. However I never did get to teach theology regularly in a faculty of theology, at least not in my own country. I was confined to giving theology courses—from which in fact I benefited greatly—to students in other faculties, which meant that the presentation had to be less specialised and within the broad scope of the relation between faith and culture.

In fact, as a priest, my whole time was taken up by pastoral work, which I enjoyed very much. At first I worked with university students and then, through this work, I came more and more into contact with the working class and the poor, until a certain fusion took place between these two mutually challenging and complementary pastoral areas. Thus I was led by events to a way of doing theology which I had not foreseen in my student years.

(b) The poor with their deprivations and their richness burst into my life. This is a people suffering from injustice and exploitation but whose faith at the same time goes very deep. Work with what could generically be called basic ecclesial communities, a term expressing this entry of the poor into the Church, placed me in contact with a world in which, in spite of its being a re-encounter with my own roots, I feel I am merely taking my first steps. Moreover as time passes, I see that the advances I have made are even more timid than I thought a few years ago.

Working in this world and becoming familiar with it, I came to realise, together with others, that the first thing to do is listen. Listen endlessly to the human and religious experiences of those who have made the sufferings, hopes and struggles of this people their own. Listen, not condescendingly, but to learn about the people and to learn about God. The lesson learnt is simple: in the dialogue of a Christian community there is no account of experience without there being an element of reflection, a way of seeing life and faith, contained in it. In what is called life reviewing—a method adopted by many communities—the perspective of faith does not only appear when the effort is made to understand certain experiences in the light of a biblical text. Life in the community means faith translated into active involvement, hope expressed in a particular attitude to life. Reflection on faith can and should expressly try to go deeper, but it also accompanies all Christian activity within a people struggling to affirm their human dignity and their condition as children of God. Sometimes, as well as talk, there is also writing about an experience of God, which has become prayer and reflection. It is impossible to do theology from the standpoint of our world without taking into account these testimonies, which are becoming more abundant every day.

This way of working led us to discover—and Puebla recognised this strongly—the 'evangelising power of the poor'. This capacity possessed by the poor to be the subject of the Gospel message carries with it a 'theologising' potential. These are not empty words or an attempt at artificial symmetry. It is a challenging daily experience which reformulates the whole question of what theology should be doing. Perhaps it makes us return to the sources, to the first efforts to understand faith in the Church's life, in the service of its task of proclaiming the Gospel, together with those whose function is to lead it by their pastoral and magisterial ministry.

It seemed clear to me that this reflection by communities who evangelise—i.e. proclaim the Gospel—and who are called together as a church (ecclesia: and that is precisely why they are 'ecclesial') is doing theology, thinking about the faith, the Christian condition. This is the exercise of the right to think possessed by the poor. It is a means of affirming their right to life, a right that in many different ways they are denied. The faith of the poor needs to understand itself, for its own sake. Fundamentally, this is an expression of the traditional principle 'fides quaerens intellectum'. The true subject of this reflection is not the isolated theologian, but the Christian community and, rippling out in concentric circles, the whole Church with its different charismata and responsibilities.

Those Christians whom we call theologians in the stricter sense ('professional theologians', as they are called in some places) will do their work effectively to the extent that they are linked to the Christian community, of which they are part and in which they daily share with others the reasons for their hope. It is definitely not a matter of being present to receive the questions asked by the poor and those involved with them in order to answer them on our own account. The task is more complex. Sharing these reflections teaches us that they contain not only questions but also answers which these Christians are discovering for themselves to the challenges they face in their solidarity with the poor and oppressed. Liberation theology has to deal with many expressions and categories which come from the basic communities (one of them, for example, is that we mentioned earlier, the evangelising power of the poor).

Thus the task of theologian is to contribute to the community what an academic education could have given it in the way of a better knowledge of and familiarity with Holy Scripture, the tradition and teaching of the Church, and contemporary theology. Theology is not an individual task, it is an ecclesial function. It is done from the Word of God received and experienced in the Church, and for the sake of its proclamation to every human being and especially the disinherited of this world. I believe that the need for solidarity with the struggle of the poor to construct a free and just human society and to proclaim the Gospel in the heart of our understanding of the faith, is not merely a necessary condition for what is sometimes called 'committed theology'. I also think it is necessary—although this is sometimes overlooked—in order to achieve a discourse on the faith which deals with the true and most vital questions for the modern world, in which the basic communities live and bear witness. Finally, it is the necessary condition for the creation of a serious, scientific and responsible theology.

In fact, contrary to what some people think—and fear—experience shows that closeness to the basic communities enforces a strict rigour upon the task of theology. The questions and the broad lines of response which come from them, their requirements for action, their work in the popular environment to which they belong, leave no room for evasive or irresponsible burblings. They require theology which is committed both to the place and to making sense of a—very necessary—reflection upon the faith.

(c) Theology understood thus is not free from tensions. For example, how to reconcile belonging to a community with its daily demands with intellectual work which also has its laws and requires its own space and time? How can one undertake a laborious effort to understand the faith when the poor face immediate needs necessary to their physical survival, with all that this implies for their lives as Christians. These questions arise and must be coped with every day.

If we are frank, we have to admit that these questions remain open. We do not manage to solve them satisfactorily; we know, for one thing, that we cannot surrender either side. Anyway, despite everything, does it really matter whether we reach a definitive answer to such questions? Is this not precisely a tension which sets up a discourse on the faith which is really helpful to the Church's work of preaching the Gospel—in word and deed? Might the anxiety that such tension sometimes produces not be a result of the uneasiness felt by the theologian who feels torn in half, although this state is a necessity both for theology itself and, more importantly, for the Christian community within which and for whose sake this intellectual work is done at all?

Neither can these questions be given a peremptory answer. Perhaps they will gradually resolve themselves—or disappear—on the way. It is a different way from the one we foresaw, when as students we felt we had a vocation to do theology. But it keeps what is good in the old way, values what we learn on our journey and shows us ancient anxieties in a new perspective. Thus we seek and make a language about God (that is, a theology) together with a people living the faith in the midst of a situation of injustice and exploitation which is a denial of God. Their sufferings are accompanied by an unquenchable hope of joy and by love in solidarity with society's poorest and most deprived. A contemplative language whose starting point is prayerful silence in the presence of God's mystery. A prophetic language which sees Christ as the unbreakable link between the kingdom and the disinherited of this world. A language sprouting in the popular sectors of Latin America and other continents, as in the book of Job, from the experience of innocent suffering. A voice which has the right to be heard, among others, within the universal Church. A theology seeking to become a hermeneutic of the hope of the poor in the God of life.

There are many methodological points needing critical determination if we are not to become trapped in superficial enthusiasms and facile formulae. But we are convinced that something profound is happening, pregnant with consequences. Only through the following of Jesus, through spirituality, is it possible to create a fruitful discourse on the faith. In it we seek a way to the Father, life in accordance with the Spirit. It is a path beaten by utter faithfulness to the demands of the poor people's world and to the Church called to proclaim the Lord's Resurrection, a message of abundant life in the midst of the death to which the poor are condemned. A way of living and thinking about the faith in relation to what John XXIII called the Church which belongs to all, and in particular, the Church of the poor.

Translated by Dinah Livingstone

Carlos Zarco Mera
Leonor Tellería
Carlos Manuel Sánchez

The Ministry of Coordinators in the Popular Christian Community (*Comunidad Christiana Popular*)

1. THE VOCATION AND THE MISSION OF AN ANIMATOR IN THE COMMUNITY
CARLOS ZARCO MERA

(a) How I came to be an animator

I joined a Basic Ecclesial Community just as anybody else would and I have now been six years in these communities. These particular communities were started off by some seminarians then they went off and after that they came back only once a week. After seven weeks, I ended up as animator of my community. When all this began, there were four communities but after the seminarians left and the priest lost interest, the communities began to disintegrate and, eventually, there were only the coordinators left and so we decided to form one community amongst ourselves. After three years we again began to establish other communities and by now we knew for certain that the priest was not with us. Today, just as at the very beginning, there are four communities and I am in charge of one of them.

(b) My work as an animator

Previously, I simply used to go along to the community and that was it. We sometimes organised some activity and we all took part in it. Nowadays, my work has increased since I am in charge of a community. Today, for instance, I have a meeting with other animators to prepare the topic for discussion and another meeting in which we come together as representatives of communities from different parts of the city; there are, of course, other complications that arise from time to time.

I wish to make it quite clear that all of these meetings are necessary in order to ensure that our work is progressing according to the Gospel and that it answers the needs of our people. In these coordinators' meetings we evaluate and examine our work in the light of the word of God in order to improve our work; it is quite a responsibility to be in charge of a community and we have to serve with all out strength and all our minds.

In meetings with my own community I have the responsibility of ensuring that the aim of the meeting is accomplished. Of course, I don't do everything. At any meeting, we share out the various activities, for instance, the time-keeper, the one who prepares the prayer, the one in whose house we meet . . . etc. Each week, we take turns in doing these things. I am acting as animator for the present but, through time, this task will also become someone else's responsibility.

When there are specific things going on in the neighbourhood or when there is a particular problem to be solved, we all take our share of the tasks in hand.

We call all of these tasks a form of service because that is precisely what they are and, in addition, in this capitalist society, almost all those who have some responsibility or some kind of power, use it to take advantage of their brothers and sisters. Now, we know that being a coordinator gives us a measure of power and the temptation of using our authority in order to acquire some personal advantage is always there, and for that reason we insist that any responsibility must be seen as a service to the community; moreover, since we are Christians and followers of Christ, we are obliged, like him, to serve and not to be served.

As an animator, I also have the task of getting to know each member of the community as well as possible. At meetings, I have to direct things in such a way that everyone gets his or her say and contributes to the discussion so that we come to some sort of conclusion regarding the problem under review; and in order to accomplish this task well I must know each brother and sister as well as possible; I must also do so in order to grow to love each member of the community. For this reason, I visit them in their own homes as well as meeting them formally as I have described.

(c) Some reflections on my work as an animator

(i) Being an animator is a vocation

In the Bible there is a passage that reads: 'Then Jesus went up into the hills and called to him those whom he desired; and they came to him . . .' (Mark 3:13). I sincerely believe that Jesus called me, that he chose me and that I have given him an affirmative response; of course, this means that I have to be pure in heart, I often fall into sin and I know that I am a sinner but I believe that, even so, Jesus still calls me. God has taken me from amongst my own people so that I can bring his word to my brothers and sisters. I never imagined that I would ever become what I am today. When I start to think about this, it becomes quite clear to me that it is due to God's grace alone that I find myself where I am today. He has called me and I respond to his invitation as best I can. Only he could have brought about this change in me.

(ii) Being an animator is a mission

God has called me for a purpose; God does not call in vain. When he speaks to us, he is calling us to action, he is calling us to get on our way. Our principal mission is that of establishing the Kingdom of God. This is a difficult mission because a large number of powerful people will not allow it and want to hinder us. At times, they bring false accusations against us; for instance, they accuse us of being led by Communists; they sometimes threaten us with imprisonment or with death and they carry out many of these threats, but that will not deter us. There are people in the Church itself who do not want us to go on; they believe that we are being used but, the fact of the matter might be that they are afraid of losing their privileges and their power. They do not understand that all we want to do is to live the Gospel totally because we know that only in this way is real happiness to be found for all men. God is with us in this mission of trying to fill the world with justice, truth and love in the midst of so many difficulties and joys. My role as animator has to do with this mission.

(iii) *Being an animator is being a servant*

As I have already said, being an animator is a form of service. In a discussion that we had, we agreed that there are three main areas of service that we must fulfil:

– first, the service of the community. This means helping the community to grow and to mature, to clarify its mission and to increase in love and justice;

– secondly, the service of unity and organisation. It is not enough to help the community to mature, it is also necessary to promote the unity and the organisation of our brothers and sisters who are struggling for the creation of a new society. We also have contacts with other organisations of the people. Some political formation (*formación política*) is necessary in this field so as not to act ingenuously and so as to avoid being used for other purposes. The great strength on which we, the poor, can rely is our own power and organisation. Moreover, united and organised is the best way of living the Kingdom of God to the fullest.

– the service of God and of our brothers and sisters. Jesus says that the whole law is summed up in loving God and one's neighbour. As an animator, this is something that I have to live out completely because there is no use in my speaking a lot about love if I do not practise what I preach.

(d) My relationship with the priest

As I said at the very beginning, the parish priest gave us no support and so we had to work on our own and without his help. He told us that he believed that we were under the control of some Communist cell since we had so much to say about politics. This hurt us a great deal because we knew that he was levelling false accusations at us; however, we just went on with things. During a retreat that we made together we saw that Jesus had entrusted to us as well his message and that we were not going to leave this entirely in the priest's hands as he was not making the best use of his own responsibility. So, we decided to forge ahead without his support; we knew that God was with us. At first, we broke off contact with him, but we realised that this was not a Christian way of behaving since he too was one of our brothers and we had to help him as well. Nowadays, we know priests and bishops who travel the same path as ourselves and this gives us a lot of encouragement. We always give notice to our parish priest of what we are doing and we invite him to join us, so far he has not come to any of our activities but we hope that some day he will join us and that he will understand that it is God who gives us strength and inspires us in this work of creating a new society.

1. THE HUMBLE OFFICE OF COORDINATOR
LEONOR TELLERÍA

I give this testimony as a member of a Christian community to which I have belonged for several consecutive years.

I shall begin by giving a brief account of how I came to join a Christian community away back about 1970. A neighbour invited me to go to a meeting with a Spanish priest who had newly arrived in the parish of St Paul the Apostle—the neighbourhood of Ducalí, to which I belong, forms part of this parish. I went to the meeting and I met this nice-looking young priest who treated us as equals; we discussed things of general interest and we were very impressed and keen to go to the next meeting. Soon, we began to study a short course of Initiation into the Christian Life and at the end of the course we met at a retreat house. This was a marvellous meeting and one that I shall never forget; there was one particular experience which I have special reason for remembering—the welcome that they gave us in one small church. When the bus that brought us there came to a halt, the doorway of the church was all joy, congratulations and affectionate greetings. A poor lady embraced me happily and congratulated me. They looked on us as if we had come from heaven and in fact I now think that we had just come from talking with God. And that is when I made my commitment. We just had to show all these people that we had come ready for work, that the seed had fallen on good ground and that the strength of their moral support would produce good fruit.

My testimony as a coordinator or animator in the community? Well, I don't think that I have done very much. I have acted best as animator when it has been my turn to give some talk; for instance, when I gave a talk on marriage and another on the Church. I believe that my best contribution to the community, in this sense, is my constancy and my desire to be just another member of the community, to give my time to the problems of other people and to forget about my own. I have not been very successful in this business of being a coordinator. I don't like imposing myself, I prefer everyone to do as they think best. I accept any direction that I am given and I do not get upset on that account. I regret that I am not able to give enough time to the community because of my many preoccupations at home. I have so much to do at home that I almost always arrive late for meetings and perhaps that is the reason for my failures as a coordinator or animator of the group.

I like to listen carefully to other people's opinions. When it is my turn to speak, I keep things short; well, it has been my own experience that having to listen to others talking at length can be boring.

There is a great deal of unity in our meetings. We discuss all sorts of topics: politics, economics, culture, social problems and, of course, religion. We always have a biblical reading followed by a commentary. At these meetings, we experience occasions of real fraternity.

We are very fortunate to have this nun with us: she is very capable and very helpful in any problem we might have. When she cannot be with us because of some pressing difficulty, she asks me to go early to the meeting so as to chair it. And that is my role in the community—to attend meetings so that they can take place.

I have a very good relationship with the clergy and with religious. When something special has been going on in the parish, for instance, the arrival of the Archbishop on a pastoral visit, they asked me to welcome him and I was very pleased to do so and I played an active role along with the priest in all that had to be done. The sisters of the Sacred Heart of Jesus, who have a house in my neighbourhood, have asked me to take part in some of their celebrations, for instance, the centenary of the foundation of the Institute, and I was very pleased to take part in that celebration and I spoke about their foundress, St Frances Xavier Cabrini. They have invited me to other special occasions of prayer which I have been delighted to attend.

I live out my faith very positively. I believe in everything and in everybody. My faith tells me that I have to make it known by serving others disinterestedly. So as to strengthen my own faith, I spent quite some time visiting other neighbourhoods that needed religious help. I used to go along with other members of the community to hold Celebrations of the Word, to give what we could to others, to spend some time with them, accepting their faith so as to unite it to our own. My faith also tells me that I have to be constant in giving my monthly pre-baptismal talks. And I take full advantage of these opportunities to talk to parents and god-parents about the very important topic of our salvation, in which our faith plays such an important part—but, a faith of life and action, and not one of words. True faith is the faith that we make known on each step along life's journey, in living itself and in our death. It is the kind of faith that seasons without destroying the taste and that sheds light without blinding.

3. COMMUNITIES COMMITTED TO LIBERATION
CARLOS MANUAL SÁNCHEZ

I am 26 years old and I have been a member of a community for seven years. Previously, I belonged to a catechumenate community. My whole family belonged to that community. I felt that it was very important to play an active part within that community in order to be a practising Christian. Everything went very well till the political situation worsened and the assassinations carried out by the Somocist dictatorship began to increase. The persecution got worse. Then, as Christians, we could not be indifferent to the suffering being endured at that time by so many of our brothers and sisters. And so, with the help of the gospels, we began to bring some light to bear on the outrages being perpetrated against the people. We would meet and choose readings and reflect on what was going on at the time. For instance, we found a lot of help in the Book of Exodus. But many people said that all this was too political. These people failed to understand that it was for the good of all the people and that it helped to clarify the difficulties that we were experiencing.

At the time, my parish priest was the one in charge of the catechumenate communities. When he discovered what we were thinking, he told me that I would be better to leave the catechumenate community and now become a member of a Basic Ecclesial Community— a more open community; other Jesuit priests who lived in Los Brasiles (a neighbouring town) would help us.

In the Basic Ecclesial Communities, our work was now much more difficult; we were being watched. This Christian work was being persecuted because of the way we denounced the outrages being committed against the people.

In open revolt, we prayed in private homes. We did not pray in churches because we were not allowed to do so. We also tried to keep ourselves informed and to inform others of any news that we managed to get. And so, in this way, we always fulfilled our Christian commitment even in the midst of war. We helped to give medical assistance when circumstances demanded it, and we gave refuge to those who had been condemned in churches and other places of worship.

Since the success of the revolution, our work has been quite different and, to a certain extent, it has become easier because of the freedom that we now enjoy. I, personally, feel a serious commitment to the establishment of the Kingdom about which Jesus Christ talks so frequently in the gospels. I joined a Basic Ecclesial Community for that very reason. These communities are better organised. All the communities in Managua work in unison and I represent one of them. And, as Christians, we members of these communities have committed ourselves to working within the people's organisations (*las organizaiciones del pueblo*). I take an active part in these organisations of the people because, as a Christian, I believe that our Christian participation is crucial in ensuring that our Revolution follows a path that will continue to benefit our people (*nuestro pueblo*). We also actively participate because we believe that in the New Nicaragua we will be able to renew mankind. We know that it is not easy, but we are prepared to sacrifice our very lives, as Our Lord Jesus Christ did and as so many of our brothers and sisters have done—whether they were Christians or claimed not to believe in God, but they have left us an example.

As a Christian, I also work for the Commission for the Promotion of Youth. The Basic Communities of Young Christians also come under its aegis. My responsibility is to visit the communities in the southern sector of the country. We encounter many problems in this pastoral work with young people since everything is so new; we have to find our own ways of doing our work effectively. For example, we find this problem in our work; we are up against an ideologically imperialist movement which is represented by a vast number of sects which have invaded our country, I refer to the pro-North American sects and not to the Protestant denominations in general. Another problem that we come across is the way in which a certain section of our own Catholic Church manipulates religion so as to confuse our young people and prevent them organising themselves within the revolution and playing their part in the work to be done. The aim of this sector of the Church is to maintain its own capitalist way of life and it turns a deaf ear to the plights of the people. Some of the young people who are aware of what's going on cease being members of the Young Christian Communities and dedicate their energies only to working for the revolution. Our task is to make quite clear that we are Christians as well and that we are working to establish the kind of new society that Christ spoke about. I, too, am young and at times I, too, get discouraged when I see how Christ is being used in the defence of personal privileges. But I believe in God and I have to follow him.

I forgot to mention that I am also in charge of a new community which has just started off. I enjoy working in this community and enjoy the Gospel reflections that we engage in. The problem is that as all the members are new to this kind of thing, I have to teach the Gospel in a more traditional way. These people cannot be brought face to face with the important events which are happening in our country, they would just say that it was all politics and they would leave. We are moving slowly but we are going ahead. As you can see, Christian work can be quite difficult.

At the moment, Nicaragua is going through a very difficult phase both economically and militarily on account of the penetration of counter-revolutionaries, the blockades and the threats of invasion. Now, we young committed Christians are prepared to take up arms if necessary—with the strength and the spirit that Christ gives us—to go on with our work of creating the new man. All this began on 19 July when we were able to open a doorway towards the establishment of the Kingdom of God here in our own Free Nicaragua.

When the Revolution gives land to the poorest peasant, when schools are built which will teach the unlettered and stop them being exploited, when Health Centres have been built for the good of the people, when enough provisions exist so that we can all eat—even if it is not very much provided that it is evenly distributed, when enough housing is built to provide each of us with a place to sleep, when the people can participate in the Council of State with a voice and a vote; when all this happens, will it not perhaps be like the primitive Christian communities which are described for us in the Acts of the Apostles? Is this not perhaps what Christ came to tell us about? Well, for all this, we Christians are prepared to defend our New Nicaragua. Many have already given their lives as Christ did. He did so out of love and we, too, are prepared to give our lives out of love for our people. We are not fighting to increase our territorial boundaries. We are fighting in order to live, in order to build up a new society.

As for myself, nobody has compelled me to join any organisation, but the Gospel itself demands that I join in order that I too share and live with my brothers and sisters.

Translated by John Angus Macdonald

Casiano Floristán

The Models of the Church which Underlie Pastoral Action

THERE HAS always been a close relationship between any particular ecclesial model and its corresponding pastoral activity.[1] This is a logical consequence since the subject of pastoral action is the *ekklesia* and the purpose of pastoral activity has frequently been understood to be the building up of the Church in the contemporary world. The *reality* within which believers function and *theology*, conceived as an understanding of the faith, are the two factors which directly influence pastoral activity and they also play a decisive role in the theological understanding and theological consciousness of the Church.

1. THE ECCLESIOLOGICAL STRUCTURAL BASIS OF PASTORAL THEOLOGY

Throughout the course of the development of pastoral or practical theology since its recognition as a university discipline in the Vienna of Maria Theresa of Austria in 1774, it has become evident that pastoral theology needs an ecclesiological basic structure.[2] It must be noted that, initially, this new discipline considered pastoral action as just another aspect of a priest's work. Towards the end of the eighteenth century, J. M. Sailer (1751–1832), who was influenced by the Enlightenment, tried to renew pastoral theology from a scriptural basis and tried to give it a theological orientation founded on revelation and on the life of faith, but his work was not taken up by others. In 1841, the brilliant disciple of J. A. Möhler and J. B. Hirscher, A. Graf, gave pastoral theology a clearly ecclesiological orientation to the extent that he defined theology as the Church's critical self-awareness[3] Many pastoralists consider him to be the real fore-runner of modern Catholic pastoral theology, just as Fr. Schleiermacher (1768–1834) was within the Protestant religion. Unfortunately, Graf's own followers went back to the earlier understanding of pastoral theology, which was practical, prescriptive and clerical. This utilitarian conception of pastoral theology was what continued in vogue till the time of the Second World War.

In Tübingen, about 1942, F. X. Arnold (1898–1969) began to study the history and nature of pastoral action. Faithfully following the best pastoral traditions of Tübingen and in close harmony with 'kerygmatic theology', Arnold chose as his point of departure the incarnation—the theandrical beginning of the human—divine relationship. The process of salvation is divine; the person of Jesus Christ is there in the very origin of the Church's activity. The Church has an intermediary role which itself is both personal and

71

instrumental. The subject responsible for pastoral action is not just the priest but the whole Church.[4]

At the same time as Arnold was working in Germany, in France, the Dominican P.-A. Liégè (1922–1979) was developing a purely ecclesiological concept of pastoral action. He defined pastoral theology as the 'theological science of ecclesial action' or of 'the mission of the Church in action' and he understood ecclesial action as 'the action of Christ in the Church, in virtue of his mission'.[5]

Practical theology is the theme of many of the writings of Karl Rahner and amongst these the *Handbuch der Pastoraltheologie* is outstanding; this work was inspired by him and completed by an extensive group of pastoralists.[6] The purpose of this work was to define the theological foundations of pastoral action and to show how the activity of the Church is developed within that context. It has been said that this handbook is a 'politology of the Church' or an 'existential ecclesiology'.[7] According to Rahner, practical theology 'is concerned with the activity by which the Church expresses itself in fact and has to express itself in any given situation. Its concern is to give theological clarification to the situation that prevails in any given instant and the situation in which the Church has to express itself at all its levels'.[8]

This understanding of pastoral action as ecclesial action founded on a practical theology of the Church was a positive achievement in the process of giving shape to a complete pastoral theology or the so called 'integrated pastoral theology'. It also served to correlate the three ecclesial actions which correspond to the classical authorities of teaching, sanctifying and governing in a way that completely reflects conciliar thinking and that did so in terms of a new vocabulary and a renewed content: the prophetic ministry or the ministry of the word, the ministry of the liturgy or of celebration and the hodegetic ministry or the ministry of charity. But during this period of time when ecclesiologies derived from the Council abounded, a certain amount of exaggerated value was given to the actual nature of the Church and its task.

During the sixties, there emerged the basic communities, forms of political theology and the theology of hope became popular, biblical hermeneutics became important, after Medellín (1968) the theology of liberation came to the fore in conjunction with new ways of analysing popular catholicism (*catolicismo popular*) and social realities and 'ascendant christologies' gave a special status to the poor—and all of this contributed to the forming of new models of pastoral action throughout the seventies. In practice, the word 'Church' was increasingly being replaced by the word 'community' with a new emphasis on the Kingdom of God being found in following Jesus Christ with the possibility of liberation from injustices being found within a Christian movement which was essentially prophetic. All of this led to ecclesial pluralism and a variety of models of pastoral action. The contribution that the theology of liberation, so called, made to Catholic theology during this period was most significant.[9]

2. ECCLESIAL AND PASTORAL MODELS

(a) Christianising pastoral policy—missionary pastoral policy

A very basic ecclesial source of tension which corresponds to the binomial *christianising Church—missionary Church*, was formulated by missionary theologians and pastoralists before the Council; this tension was lived out in the flesh by worker priests, by nuns working in shanty towns and by secular 'apostolic movements' and it was epitomised by the dictum 'read the gospels according to the signs of the times'.[10]

Between the years 1935–1955, there occurred throughout the Catholic world, but particularly in the Church in France, a most important revival of ecclesial and apostolic activity. During this time, a rich and varied vocabulary came into being which is represented by concepts like 'evangelisation', 'community', 'testimony', 'compromise', etc. and this happened within the *eschatology–incarnation* dialectic[11] which was, itself, the consequence of two theological schools of thought which preceded the Council[12]

Before the Council, the Church could be identified in terms of an unequal society, a priestly patrimony, a sacramental establishment, an alliance with power bases, an inflexible morality, orthodoxy in teaching and uniformity in action; in the post-conciliar period, there emerges a Church which can be identified in terms of a community, which is founded on a brotherhood of faith, witness and the incarnation, is committed to the poor and the disinherited, is orthodox in its activity and is open to social reality from the perspectives of communion/*koinonia*. The writings which describe these two pastoral positions are very numerous. In this regard, there exists the dispute between kerygmatic theology and scholastic theology, and between those who lay greater emphasis on large numbers rather than minorities, on conventional Catholicism rather than one of conviction, on sacrament rather than prophecy, on charism rather than institution, on infant baptism rather than adult baptism, etc.

One important example to consider in regard to the conflict between a christianising pastoral policy and a missionary pastoral policy is to be found in *Líneas pastorales en América Latina* by G. Gutiérrez.[13] He reviews four pastoral models: a christianising pastoral, one of new christianity, one of maturity in the faith and one of prophetic action. After presenting the characteristics of each kind, G. Gutiérrez acknowledges that each is being put into effect in South America 'at differing levels of extension and realisation' while the christianising pastoral policy is 'the most prevalent'.

Catholic sociologists, particularly in the Spanish-speaking parts of the Church, have likewise clearly delineated classifications of ecclesial and pastoral models which are at odds with one another: a Catholicism of the people, a cultural Catholicism, a non-institutional Catholicism and an ecclesial Catholicism (*catolicismo popular, cultural, no institucionel y ecclesial*).[14] They have also identified models which they define as 'ideal types' which have succeeded one another historically: viz; total Catholicism, a personal religiosity and a religion of commitment.[15] Others make a distinction between a Catholicism of the masses which demands no commitment and a renewed Catholicism which demands commitment.[16] There is no lack of analyses of kinds according to ideology, social class and political function and these find concrete expression in four basic tendencies; Catholic nationalism, reformist centralism, suppressed Catholicism and the critico-prophetic Church.[17]

Others reduce the models of the Church to three: the integrist or 'bunker' Church, the open Church or the Church of the 'aggiornamento' and the Church of the people or non-integrated Church (*popular o no integrada*),[18] and to each of these basic types corresponds a form of pastoral action: the traditional, the renewed traditional and the community-group forms.[19]

In South America, the models of the Church which demand different pastoral approaches are reduced by C. Boff to two basic forms. In the first place, there is the christianising model which is one of continuity and is centred on the parish; it is pyramidal in structure, with up-dated ecclesial expressions, and practises its religion through the clerical ministry and is allied with the bourgeoisie. The other model is that of the *diaspora*: it is not one of continuity and is centred on the basic ecclesial communities; it is cyclic in structure and uses innovatory ecclesial expressions, and it stresses ethical practices and acts in harmony with the popular classes.[20]

(b) Evangelisation—sacramentalisation

In a similar way and as a consequence of having differing visions of the Church, tension has emerged, time and again in the history of pastoral action, between what is evangelical and what is sacramental.[21] After the Second World War, the word–sacrament dialectic found formal expression in the binomial *evangelisation-sacraments*, and was given prominence because of the disputes between 'evangelisers' and 'sacramentalists'.

Throughout the fifties, the concept of sacrament was theologically re-vitalised from the point of departure of the faith,[22] of the category of personal encounter,[23] of the word[24] and of the sacramentality of the Church.[25] The Second Vatican Council adopted these sacramental perspectives and gave them aspects of missionary activity by describing the sacraments as signs which suppose, nurture, strengthen and express the faith.[26]

In order to avoid a kind of schizophrenic confusion of evangelising and liturgical action, the Church must act in a coherent way. The tension between evangelisation and sacraments has been analysed in many writings since the Council and there has been no lack of documentation on the subject from Episcopal Conferences.[27]

The evangelising model emphasises evangelical Christianity in which the faith is verified to the extent that it conforms with the practice of Jesus and the practice of real liberation; the worshipping model emphasises sacramental Christianity in which testimony of the faith is given in the Christian liturgical mystery. Within the former category, humanity is essentially a compromise, the Church is a prophetic community, Christ is the complete man for all others, God is a call to the establishment of his Kingdom, the faith is the practical exercise of liberation, charity is a social and political action and hope is the point of departure for the transformation of the world. Within the latter category, man is a gratuitous being, the Church is a sign of salvation, Christ is the proto-sacrament of the Father, God is overflowing love, the faith is a complete sense of life, charity is effective personal love and hope is a total trust in the promises of God.

These two ways of interpreting the reality of Christianity have recently been enriched by a re-appraisal of the evangelical nature of Christianity and of the influence that the social and political ambiences can bring to bear on the faith and the sacraments. If everything has a political dimension then it is no less true that everything has a symbolic or sacramental dimension.[28]

(c) The Church, a 'great institution' and the Church, a 'network of communities'

After the Second Vatican Council, basic ecclesial communities began to emerge in South America as new models of the Church and these found their original impetus in the five-year Overall Pastoral Plan announced by the Brazilian Bishops towards the end of 1965. At Medellín, these communities received official approval. The way in which they have spread throughout South America in conjunction with the development of liberation theology has been quite remarkable. Much has been written about their experiences, fundamental characteristics and capacity for evangelisation. Because of their importance, the National Meetings of Basic Ecclesial Communities in Brazil are here listed: (1) in 1975, *The Church which comes to life from the people* (que nace del pueblo) *through the Holy Spirit*, (2) in 1976, *The Church, a pilgrim people*, (3) in 1978, *The Church, a people which finds its own liberation*, (4) in 1981, *The Church, an oppressed people in the process of organisation for its own liberation*, and (5) in 1983, *The basic ecclesial community, seed of a new society*. Also of importance are the meetings of the Ecumenical Association of Third World Theologians which were held from 1976 to 1983.[29]

The fundamental option of the basic ecclesial model is for the people (*por el pueblo*), the poor and liberation. According to L. Boff, this model has the following characteristics; (1) It is the Church of the people, not for the people but with the people, that is, the people of God, who share a responsibility with a model of clerical Church. (2) It is a Church in communion, a community of faith and of charity, with liberating sacramental signs, engaging in dialogue, with relationships of brotherhood in the face of an imposing Church which is centred on the binomial authority-obedience. (3) Lastly, it is a liberating and prophetic Church, which commits itself socially, is conscious of human rights, brings injustices to light and defends those who are exploited in the face of a Church which has allied itself with the rich, is atrophied and only has rites and sacraments.[30]

The *ecclesiality* of the basic communities has been constantly emphasised by their representatives and has been officially recognised by the hierarchy. The basic ecclesial community is 'the original cell of ecclesial structuring' (Medellín), 'the hope of the Church' (E.N.), 'the central source of evangelisation and the driving force for liberation' (Puebla) and 'the new form of being for the Church' (Episcopal Conference of Brazil, 1983). In short, it is the transformation of the people of the poor into the people of God (*pueblo de los pobres transformado en pueblo de Dios*).

In fact, in the light of contemporary reality, R. Muñoz states that 'two distinct models of the Church function; two models that imply different locations, different mentalities and differing ways of acting. Of course, we are not dealing with models which exist, complete in themselves and in isolation from one another, but, within the one Church, they constitute two clearly distinct polarisations of its internal dynamism and social influences.[31] They constitute models of the Church which R. Muñoz defines as 'great institution' and 'network of communities'.

E. Dussel writes that the Church of communities and of the people 'is not another Church, is not a new Church, but is simply a *model* of the perennial Church.[32]

(d) Models of community pastoral policy

The phenomenon of Christian communities is neither uniform nor unitary. In fact, models vary according to their differing characteristics and objectives. There are basic areas of similarity but the ways in which communities are expressed or conceived can be quite different.

The very expression *basic community* (all of them are or try to be Christian or ecclesial) is a composition of two terms, which is both complex and profound in significance. 'When the emphasis is on the notion of *community*', states E. Dussel, 'the ecclesial focus of attention is of necessity *ad intra*' and 'when, on the other hand, the emphasis is on the notion of *basic*, the tendency is to give more importance to the *ad extra* function of the Church'.[33] This differentiation in emphasis has been highlighted by the Canadian G. Paiement who makes a distinction between *fervent* communities and *critical* communities (others describe these as 'prophetic'). Within the former category, 'interpersonal relationships' prevail, with features of fraternity, good behaviour, the word of God, prayer, mutual support as occasion demands and enthusiasm. Within the latter category, a certain kind of 'temporal or political commitment' can be noted with features of concern with structures, activity, external manifestations, liberating faith, popular theology and a critical communion with the institutional Church. A distinguishing feature of the fervent communities is their sensitivity towards the *transcendental* while a special feature of the *critical* kind is their emphasis on the incarnation.[34]

R. J. Kleiner distinguishes three kinds of Christian communities: the *communities of faith*, centred on the biblical *kerygma*; the *eucharistico-social communities* which give equal emphasis to the liturgy and to commitment and the *socio-political communities* which emphasise the Christian *diaconia* or critique, from Marxist viewpoints, in regard to religious ideology and capitalist society.[35]

Similarly, a variety of models can be distinguished in Spain and these include the neo-catechumenal kind and the charismatic and popular types which are organised on a national level and even include expansions to or connections with similar or equivalent groupings in other countries.[36] A recent document from the Spanish Episcopal Pastoral Commission recognises that in the realm of these communities certain differences are evident although collective units can be distinguished which are 'like *great families* which bring together those which have come into being, inspired by the same pastoral intuitions.'[37] The exhortation of Paul VI *Evangelii Nuntiandi* (8 December 1975) alludes to different models and belittles those which 'come together in a spirit of hostile criticism against the Church which they stigmatise as *institutional*', which adopt an 'attitude of censure and rejection of the Church's external functions', and which are 'hostile towards the hierarchy' and 'separate themselves from the Church' (No. 58).

(e) Two interpretations of a pastoral policy for the people

The so called popular pastoral policy (or pastoral policy for the people) (*pastoral popular*) came into being in South America in response to the ecclesial models represented by the *basic communities* which soon came to be called 'basic ecclesial communities' (to avoid negative criticism) and later 'popular christian communities' (to avoid ambiguities). According to J. Marins, this form corresponds to 'a basic Church and a model which is communitary, prophetic, liberating and missionary'.[38] The emphasis is on *the base*, which is understood to be the people of the poor and the oppressed (*pueblo pobre y oprimido*) and not merely a reference to a primitive cell of believers or to a personal nucleus in which the faith takes root. The base, then, is the people (*el pueblo*).

Over all, the concept of *people* (*pueblo*) is interpreted in a variety of ways, as is the adjective *popular* (*popular*). In the present article, two interpretations of the meaning of 'people' are relevant: i.e. as a nation-culture (the citizens of a country) and as a sector or as sectors of a nation, that is to say a social class (the poor and the socially peripheral).[39]

If we understand the people as the collective subject of any historical experience, with an indigenous culture, a personal religiosity, a particular morality, a distinct language or tongue and a common destiny, then a *pastoral policy of the people* will be 'an evangelisation of the culture of a people'.

On the other hand, if by people we mean the collective subject of the poor, the exploited and the peripheral in the socio-economic sense, then *a pastoral policy of the people* will be 'an evangelisation of the poor and from within the poor'.

'Both meanings of the word people', states J. C. Scannone, 'are semantically and ontologically related because we believe that the poor and the simple are those who condense and collectively reveal with ever growing clarity what is communal and common, that is to say, the wisdom and the way of life which properly belong to the historico-cultural reality that we recognize as *ourselves*. This is so because the simplicity of the simple, which has not been *a priori* immunised against outside influences is, nevertheless, not so easily disfigured by the privileges which emanate from possessions, from power and from knowledge'.[40]

Translated by John Angus Macdonald

Notes

1. A. Dulles *Modelos de la Iglesia* (Santander 1975), *Models of the Church* (New York 1973). H. Fries 'Cambios en la imagen de la Iglesia y desarrollo histórico-dogmático' *Mysterium Salutis* IV/1 (Madrid 1973) pp. 231–296.

2. See H. Schuster 'Die Geschichte der Pastoraltheologie' *Handbuch der Pastoraltheologie* (Fribourg 1964) I pp. 40–92.

3. See A. Graf *Kritische Darstellung des gegenwartigen Zustandes der praktischen Theologie* (Tübingen 1841).

4. See F. X. Arnold *Pastoraltheologische Durchblicke* (Fribourg 1965).

5. P.-A. Liégé 'Introduction' to the writings of F. X. Arnold in *Al servicio de la fe* (Barcelona 1963 2nd edn.) pp. 7–17.

6. See *Handbuch der Pastoraltheologie. Praktische Theologie der Kirche in ihrer Gegenwart* (Fribourg 1964–1972) 5 vols.

7. Similar to the scheme of the *Handbuch* (see note 6) is the work of C. Floristán and M. Useros *Teología de la acción pastoral* (Madrid 1968).

8. K. Rahner 'Die praktische Theologie im Ganzen der theologischen Disziplinen' *Die praktische Theologie zwischen Wissenschaft und Praxis* (Munich 1968) pp. 47–48. The quotation is from *Schriften sur Theologie* (Einsiedeln 1967) VIII pp. 133–139.

9. See E. Dussel *A History of the Church in Latin America. Colonialism to Liberation* (Grand Rapids, Mich. 1981); R. Oliveros *Liberación y teología. Génesis y crecimiento de una reflexión (1966–1976)* (Lima 1977); M. Manzanera *Teología y salvación-liberación en la obra de Gustavo Gutiérrez* (Bilbao 1978).

10. See P. Richard *Mort des chrétientés et naissance de l'Église* (Paris 1978). The theological and historical analysis of the christianising Church and its transition to a missionary Church was first investigated by Congar and Chenu.

11. See B. Besret *Incarnation ou eschatologie? Contribution á l'histoire du vocabulaire religieux contemporain 1935–1955* (Paris 1964).

12. See L. Malevez 'Deux théologies catholiques de l'histoire' *Bijdragen* 10 (1949) pp. 225–240.

13. Conferences given in 1964 under the direction of Catholic university movements, completed in 1967 and published in 1968. The second edition (Lima) appeared in 1967. In French: *Réinventer le visage de l'Eglise. Analyse théologique de l'évolution des pastorales* (Paris 1971). I wrote a similar analysis for Spain 'Tendencias pastorales en la Iglesia Española' *Teología y mundo contemporáneo (Homenaje a Karl Rahner)* (Madrid 1975) pp. 491–512.

14. See J. M. Marcos-Alonso *Análisis sociológico del catolicismo español* (Barcelona 1967); J. González Anleo *Catolicismo nacional: nostalgia y crisis* (Madrid 1975).

15. See A. L. Orensanz *Religiosidad popular espanola: 1940–1965* (Madrid 1974).

16. See F. Urbina *Informe F.O.E.S.S.A. 1975* (Madrid 1976) Chap. V.

17. See J. C. García *Fe y política* (Madrid 1977) pp. 11–35.

18. See J. Chao *La Iglesia en el franquismo* (Madrid 1976).

19. See J. M. Castillo 'Diversos modelos de pastoral y el problema de la pastoral de la Iglesia' *Sal Terrae* 66 (1978) 667–677.

20. See 'Puebla 78' *Ecclesia* No. 1,147 (1978) 1898. For further information on the *Church of the People* in Spain, see J. Rey and J. J. Tamayo *Por una Iglesia del pueblo* (Madrid 1976); J. M. Castillo *La alternativa cristiana. Hacia una Iglesia del Pueblo* (Salamanca 1978).

21. See C. Floristán and L. Maldonado *Los sacramentos, signos de liberación* (Madrid 1977); C. Floristán 'Sakramente und Befreiung' *Profetische Diakonie* (Vienna 1977) pp. 292–310.

22. See L. Villete *Foi et sacrement* (Paris 1959) 2 vols.

23. Cf. E. Schillebeeckx *Cristo, sacramento del encuentro con Dios*, (San Sebastian 1964); first published in Amberes 1957; English edition *Christ the Sacrament* (London 1963).

24. See K. Rahner 'Palabra y eucaristía' *Escritos de teología* (Madrid 1962) IV pp. 323–367; 'Wort und Eucharistie' *Aktuelle Fragen zur Eucharistie* ed. M. Schmaus (Munich 1960) pp. 7–52.

25. See O. Semmelroth *La Iglesia como Sacramento Original* (San Sebastian 1963); *Die Kirche als Ursakrament* (Frankfurt 1953).

26. *Sacrosanctum Concilium* No. 59.

27. See The French Episcopal Conference *Église, signe de salut au milieu des hommes* (Paris 1972), *La Iglesia, signo de salvacion en medio de los hombres* (Madrid 1976); *Une Église qui célébre et qui prie* (Paris 1974), *Una Iglesia que Celebra y que Ora* (Santander 1976); also, see *Evangelización y Sacramentos* ed. The Spanish National Liturgical Secretariat (Madrid 1973) and the Italian Episcopal Conference *Evangelizzazione, Sacramenti, Promozione umana. Le scelte pastorali della Chiesa in Italia* (Rome 1979).

28. C. Floristán and L. Maldonado, the work cited in note 21, pp. 15–19.

29. See E. Dussel 'Theologies of the "Periphery" and the "Centre": Encounter or Confrontation?' *Concilium* 171 (1984) 87–97.

30. L. Boff *Iglesia: carisma y poder. Ensayos de eclesiologia militante* (Santander 1982) p. 209.

31. R. Muñoz *Solidaridad liberadora: Misión eclesial* (Bogotá 1977) p. 32.

32. See E. Dussel et al. *La Iglesia latinoamericana de Medellin a Puebla* (Bogotá 1979); *De Medellín a Puebla* 1–111 (São Paulo 1982–1983).

33. E. Dussel 'La "base" en la teologia de la liberacion' *Concilium* 104 (Spanish ed.) (1975) p. 80.

34. See G. Paiement *Groupes libres et foi chrétienne. La signification actuelle de certains modèles de communauté* (Tournai 1972).

35. R. J. Kleiner *Basisgemeinden in der Kirche. Was sie arbeiten—wie sie wirken* (Graz 1976) pp. 190–191.

36. See C. Floristán 'Modelos de comunidades cristianas' *Sal Terrae* 67 (1979) pp. 61–72 and 145–154; The Diocesan Catechetical Secretariate of Madrid *Comunidades plurales en la Iglesia* (Madrid 1981).

37. See *Servicio pastoral de las pequeñas comunidades cristianas* (Madrid 1982).

38. See J. Marins *Modelos de Iglesia. C.E.B. en América Latina. Hacia un modelo liberador* (Bogotá 1976).

39. See L. Gera 'Pueblo, religion de pueblo e Iglesia' *Iglesia y religiosidad popular en América Latina* (Bogotá 1977) pp. 258–283. J. C. Scannone 'Culture populaire, pastorale et théologie' *Lumen Vitae* 32 (1977) pp. 21–38.

40. J. C. Scannone 'Sabiduria popular y teología inculturada' *Stomata* 35 (1979) 5.

PART III

*A Systematic Reflection on the People of God in the
midst of the Poor*

Pedro Ribeiro de Oliveira

An Analytical Examination of the Term 'People'

THE TERM 'people' (*povo*) is far from having one semantic meaning. In making an analysis of it here from a sociological viewpoint, I shall be bearing its application to the reality of the Church as the People of God continually in mind, since the point of this analysis is to help us to understand the reality of the Church, particularly that of the 'popular' Church (*Igreja 'popular'*) in Latin America. I propose to follow this procedure: first, a short examination of the term 'people' in the juridical sense; then its use as a sociological category by 'populist' regimes and popular movements, in order to discover the sociological bases for its semantic ambivalence. This analysis should then show us the sense in which it is possible to speak sociologically of a 'popular' Church.

In cultural anthropology, 'people' has the same sense as nation or ethnic group, a population defined by its pertinence to a particular culture.[1] This is clearly not the sense in which the term 'people' concerns theology, since it would make no sense to define the Church as a people culturally distinct from any other.

In social philosophy, 'a people is not any group of men brought together anyhow, but is the coming together of numbers associated by the concensus of law and by common interests', according to the classic definition of Cicero, which was taken up by St Augustine and again by Thomas Aquinas.[2] Such a definition implies reference to the State as the guardian of law and the common good, so that we find it developed in the juridical theory of the State, in which the people are 'the totality of citizens or subjects of one and the same State'.[3] In this sense, the term 'people' applied to the Church leads to the latter's definition as a *societas perfecta* with legislative, judiciary and coercive power over its subjects.[4] This, however, is not the theological implication of the use of terms such as 'the Church that is born of the people', (*Igreja que nasce do povo*) or the 'popular' Church; this Church reality does not refer to 'people' as the totality of subjects, in the juridical sense, of the Church, but to 'people' as a sociological category, and this is the sense in which I propose to analyse it here.

1. 'PEOPLE' AS A SOCIOLOGICAL CATEGORY IN 'POPULISM' (*POPULISMO*)

Social scientists try to avoid using the term 'people' as far as possible, owing to its current use in ordinary speech and the ideological charge attaching to this. Now that the modern State has made it the principal source for the legitimacy of its power, it can never be used neutrally or impartially. It is because the modern State claims that all power comes from the people and will be exercised in the name of the people that the intellectual debate about who the people are and who can speak for them is so sharp. Defining who the people are means defining who can legitimise political power.

In the midst of the whole debate, with all its semantic ambivalence, there is nevertheless one category of persons who are always included under the heading of 'people': those of humble social position. 'A hidden intuition makes everyone judge himself more of the people the lower his social condition: it is a title—and the only one—to which those least favoured by fortune will cling. They possess nothing, but on account of this they pride themselves on being the people'.[5] This is then the first element of a sociological definition of 'people'.

The second is the social polarisation between the people and the élite. In Latin America, as in most countries that have been colonised, this always emerges as a distinction between the mass of the natives, who are poor and cut off from full rights of citizenship, and the élite of those of European descent, the nobles, the cultured, the rich. Sometimes this polarisation is very clearly marked, as in the case of racial difference (the white élite as opposed to the mass of Indians or negroes), linguistic difference (the élite speak a European language, the mass use native languages and dialects) and even religious difference (the Christianity of the élite is opposed to popular religious practices which are called 'animist', 'magical' or 'superstitious'). In this polarisation, it is from the pole of the masses that the category of 'people' will emerge, taking in all the downtrodden and marginalised—those who do not count in a properly ordered society.[6]

The third constitutive element in the category 'people' is its dialectical opposition to the category 'mass'. The emergence of a people is a historical fact. While the marginalised masses of the Third World came into being through colonialisation, they only became 'peoples' once they in some way took part in a national historical project uniting all sectors in one social whole capable of acting as a historical subject. While the colonial structure remained in force, these social sectors remained 'in a mass situation, or that of a proletariat', in Toynbee's sense of the term. It is with the breakdown of the colonial structure that the people emerge, 'as a result of this out-pouring of experience common to a group at one time, experience stemming from reference to a common project and capable of overcoming the tensions and antagonisms at work in the whole'. So the 'people' can only 'come out of societies with differing social strata and in conditions of considerable dynamism on the part of their various forces and classes'.[7]

The three elements outlined above are essential in a definition of 'people' as a sociological category: it is made up of groups and classes of humble condition, socially situated at the opposite pole from the ruling élite, and it is distinguished from the mass in that it embraces different forces and classes in a common historical project. Such a definition is useful to determine the parameters of research, but it hardly solves the theoretical side of the question: the practical problem of knowing who—not what—the people are. While it would be possible to reach a consensus on this minimal definition of 'people', the debate on who is or is not included in this category with its enormous legitimising potential still obviously goes on.

In Latin America, this debate has two main frameworks: the 'populist' ('populistas') regimes of the 1950s and 1960s, and the 'popular' (populares) movements of the present. For 'populism' the term 'people' becomes assimilated to the term 'nation', with the 'people's' historical project being that of national development. While its various embodiments have different tinges—from the Marxist-Leninist formulation to the different versions of right-wing nationalism—they all agree on the central point: development is the main historical task to be carried out by a conjunction of all progressive social forces and classes, articulated by the nationalist State in opposition to the economic, political and social structures of colonialism.[8] So the 'populist' project embraced all parts of the nation, excluding only the old ruling élite which was compromised with the colonial structure and those sectors of society which supported it.

In the populist project, it was the State that undertook the historical mission of uniting all progressive social classes around the project of national development, and so while it was effectively under the control of the middle classes, it had to take on a form acceptable to the masses. This is why regimes such as those of Perón in Argentina, Vargas in Brazil, Cardenas in Mexico, Ibarras in Equador and other similar ones in Latin America are called 'populist'.[9] The suppression of these populist regimes and the advent of military regimes of 'national security' left the category of 'people' in the shade, since the military prefer to use the term 'nation', of which they see themselves as the true interpreters. The populist project, however, is still alive today, setting itself up as an alternative policy in view of the economic failure of the regimes of 'national security'. The term 'people' applied to the populist project is still in use, but is being overtaken by a new meaning coming out of the present-day popular movements. This is what we must analyse next.

2. 'PEOPLE' ('POVO') AS A TERM USED IN THE POPULAR MOVEMENT

The popular movements of opposition to the regimes of 'national security' brought with them a reappropriation of the term 'people' by the people themselves. In this there is no theoretical elaboration of the preceding type, worked out by social scientists and politicians serving the populist project, but rather an intellectual product of a popular type. Without recourse to academic theoretical refinements, the people themselves define who they are and who their enemies are, outline their own historical project, work out new forms of popular organisation, and are also responsible for an impressive range of symbolical productions—poems, songs, paintings, religious ceremonies, etc.—which express their struggles, their sufferings, their hopes and their joys. Although this intellectual and artistic output has not been studied to the extent it deserves, one can say that it contains key elements for understanding the way the people define themselves. Some of the best written expressions come from the texts prepared by the basic ecclesial communities for their national meeting in 1978.[10]

In the first place, 'people' means all those living in the poor regions, whether villages and the countryside or the slums and shanty towns of the big cities. For example: 'here is a place the people have put a lot of work into. Most of the people work for others'; 'this is where the people who have been pushed aside live, the people who build mansions and have no home fit to lay their own head in, the people who produce food and have nothing to eat, the people who make buses and have to walk'. So we are dealing with a term that designates a collectivity, the sum total of those who share the social experience of living at the unfavoured pole of society. 'People' means the poor taken as a whole, those despised by established society.

The term becomes more explicit when it is opposed by various terms referring to the ruling élite. Some examples: 'till now, the municipal authorities have never taken any notice of the poor agricultural workers'; 'the authorities in this place are the landowners'; 'the bosses rule when the people are disunited'; 'how can we influence the decisions of employers or councils when we are too weak to stand up to them?'; 'the traditional Church has no use for the people, it is afraid of the people': 'the city has some fine districts, but these are not for the people to live in; they are for the rich'; 'all this is the result of a situation brought about by the "great" '; 'there are leaders of the people on the side of the oppressor'. In all such expressions, the enemies of the people are identified as those who hold political power, who have land or capital, the police force, religious authorities—all those, in short, who effectively make up the power structure of society. They are the

G

'great', whose world is not the world of the people, the 'little' and the 'weak'. Seen in this way, the term 'people' ceases to be purely descriptive and comes to denote a social identity proper to those who are at the opposite pole from those who form the ruling classes and groups.

But this category only acquires social power when the people cease to be a mass and organise themselves in some way so as to influence their own destiny. As long as there is no popular organisation, the people will not mobilise themselves: 'it is the people themselves who don't believe in their leaders'; 'the majority of the people still think that God wants things to be like this'; 'the people know they can't do anything'; 'we are a collection of scattered remnants, not a people'. It is only when some individuals inspire this mass to fight for better living conditions that it can come out of this state of passivity and solve its problems by its own strength alone, thereby becoming a popular movement.

Popular movements can act in a variety of ways: a joint effort at house building, campaigns for improving public services in the district, campaigns for the election of genuine trade union officials, formation of local associations for the defence of citizens' rights, formation of rural district councils, smallholders' defence of property rights, mobilisation of a campaign for better health care, and many other campaigns. What is important in all of them, as the reports quoted show, is that 'the people become conscious of their rights and their dignity, move beyond individual interests for the sake of collective action, uniting and organising to face common problems and difficulties, and taking on the responsibility for controlling their own actions'. Or, as another report puts it: 'the commission saw that the basic groups had to be strengthened if the inhabitants were to be able to carry on the struggle. In the end, the struggle is the people's and without the people there can be no victory.' Popular basic groups—with the ecclesial communities prominent among them—act as catalysing agents, mobilising sectors of the population to collective action, in which process the masses become an organised people. This can be a rapid or a slower process, depending on the conditions of the place and the type of struggle, but in the end it always produces the same results: in the course of their struggles the people come to realise that by uniting and organising they gain in strength and become capable of influencing their own destiny. This is therefore a process of popular political self-education.[11]

Finally, the term people takes on an axiological dimension: the people discover their own values and work out their own historical project as something that belongs to them, not something they have to copy from the cultured and ruling élites. Some examples of this use of the term are: 'the people should always start from their interests as the common people and not from the interests of those who happen to be in power at the moment'; 'when people recognise popular wisdom, when they believe in the ordinary people, then oppression is cut off at the roots'; 'the people's way of acting, of addressing one another, is different from that of the upper classes'; 'the people will stop being puppets in the power struggle and will decide their own destiny'. At this stage in popular consciousness, the people not only feel themselves to be a people, but that this is a good thing to be. Their values, their culture, their art, their religious expressions, are no longer seen as inferior to those of the élite and become a motive for pride in the people. Belonging to the people, behaving like the people, with the aesthetic sensibility of the people and the religion of the people, is no longer a dishonour or shame; on the contrary, it becomes a motive of pride for a people who identify themselves as different from the élite and with their own values. We have now come a long way from the concept of a people as everyone of the same nationality. This is what we must examine next.

3. THE HISTORICAL AND SOCIOLOGY FRAMEWORK OF THE TERM 'PEOPLE' (*POVO*)

Comparing the meaning of 'people' in the populist project and in the present-day popular movement, what emerges clearly is its eminently historical character. Yet while both use the same word, its meaning is very different in the populist context and in that of the popular movement. It is true that in both cases it refers to a collectivity greater than one social class, a collectivity marked by preferential reference to those least favoured in society, distinguished from a mere mass by the conjunction of social classes and forces round a common historical project. In the populist concept, however, this common project is national development led by the State, and therefore under the hegemony of the middle classes, since they are the ones who hold political power. In the concept of the popular movement, on the other hand, the historical project implies a break with the capitalist system and the building of a new society, led not by the State, but by the popular movements themselves within civil society. In the first, power belongs to the bourgeoisie, who hold State office; in the second, it belongs to the popular classes and their organisations acting on civil society.

In any discussion of the meaning of the term 'people' today, one has to refer to the sociological context in which it emerges. The populist project framework gives pride of place to the idea of the people as nation, while the popular movement framework lays stress on the idea of the people as the totality of the oppressed classes.[12] The ambivalence of the term 'people', however, goes beyond the semantic order into the sociological order: there it expresses the real divergence between two different historical projects and therefore the divergence between the intellectuals belonging to the bourgeoisie and those belonging to the popular classes. When we use the term in one or the other sense, we are placing ourselves within one or the other framework of reference. Therefore, by taking up the definition of the people given by the popular movement, we are taking up a stance that implies seeing the reality of the Church in Latin America from the standpoint of the oppressed classes. This is what we shall examine in the last section of this article.

4. 'POPULAR' CHURCH AS A SOCIOLOGICAL CATEGORY

The 'popular' Church appears in the dialectical process of constituting a people from the masses, as one of the mediators of this process. It cannot be analysed apart from this process, since it is not only an ecclesial fact, but also a social and political fact in the widest sense of the term.

The emergence of the people from the masses is not a phenomenon arising spontaneously from the masses. Besides the conjunction of economic, political and social conditions which either help or hinder the process, there is a decisive factor which is the intervention of catalysing agents, capable of mobilising sectors of the masses into a popular movement. In populist regimes, these agents were normally agents of the State itself, or political parties associated with the populist project. In the case of present-day popular movements, these catalysing agents are small popular groups already existing within the masses, such as residents' associations, Christian communities, old people's clubs, youth groups, working people's groups, tenants and smallholders' associations, etc. It is by encouraging and supporting these groups, through the basic ecclesial communities and 'specialised pastoral missions'—to workers, peasants, Indians, young people, women, etc.—that the Church becomes a social agent of the popular movement, acting as one of the mediators of the process of forming a people. We must not, however, lose sight of the fact that the Church (and by this I mean all the Christian churches that are at work in the popular field) is only one of several institutions exercising this mediating function, alongside political parties, trade unions and other bodies that go to make up the social fabric.

There are two dialectical facets to this insertion of the Church in the popular movement. The first is that of the impact made by the Church in the process of forming a people. There is no doubt that the Christian churches are leaving their mark on this process. The most obvious example is the Sandinista revolution in Nicaragua: while this is by no means an example of neo-Christendom, it does show the deep mark that Christianity has made on the revolutionary process. The presence of Christianity is obvious in the ethic that inspires the political practice of the people, in the project of building a new society and even in the symbolism used. It is not so much a confessional presence as one of values and symbols which have impregnated the Christians taking part in the revolutionary process and are handed on through their political and symbolical practices.

The other dialectical facet of this insertion of the Church in the popular movement is the impact of the active presence of the people in the Church. It is not only the Church that has opted for the poor; there is also the inverse movement, of the poor who opt for the Church.[13] It is true that in Latin America the poor have always been in the Church, but their presence was an anonymous and passive one. They received the sacraments, learned the catechism, but took no effective part in the life of the Church, except as 'the faithful' at religious services. Today the participation of the poor in the Church has taken on a new form. In the basic Christian communities, or evangelical communities, or specialised pastoral groups, and even in parish and diocesan assemblies, the people are now no longer an anonymous mass of 'faithful', but a group of Christians organised in their local communities and therefore capable of playing an active part in the life of the Church. In this way the people are leaving their mark on the central aspects of Church life, and the Church is taking on the form, the purpose, the way of life and the style of the people.

Taking part in an act of worship at one of the basic ecclesial communities is enough to make one appreciate the style that the people are imposing on the Church. There we will not find the ascetic, rational style of bourgeois Catholicism, but the boisterous, lively style of popular Catholicism. The people have brought their cultural baggage into the Church, and so can feel at ease in its worship and assemblies. We will not find there the atmosphere of recollection in which each soul finds itself alone before God, but the festive atmosphere in which the whole community together celebrates by bringing its problems, struggles and joys into God's presence. In place of the monotonous repetition of prayers following pre-established formulas, there are spontaneous prayers accompanied by songs, poems and physical expression, combined with a rediscovery of popular religious traditions previously condemned as 'superstitious'. In short, the people have brought to the Church their way of expressing themselves and relating to one another and to God. In doing so, they have conferred a popular form on the Church, just as the feudal nobility once gave it an aristocratic form and the bourgeoisie a bourgeois style.[14]

And it is not only in the cultural sense that one can speak of a popular Church. In the particular case of the Catholic Church, the basic communities as a form of Church presence in the popular movement are having an effect on the very structure of the ecclesiastical institution. As it is, built around a clerical axis, with all power of decision-making in the hands of the clergy, with its basic unit as the parish, the present ecclesiastical structure in bourgeois society has no place for the base communities. Built on principles of communion and participation, these require the presence of priest or bishop not as holders of decision-making powers, but as focal points of unity in the Church and of fidelity to the Gospel. Parochial organisation itself, centred on the person of the parish priest, is giving way before the vitality of the basic communities, which link up with one another through means of meetings and assemblies without reference to the parish bureacracy. The experience of community in the popular movement, where no one has perpetual control, where solidarity is the basic principle, where decisions are taken in common, where all are equally valued, is being transposed into the ecclesiastical institution, with direction of a collegiate character taking the place of bureacratic direction, with the full participation of the basic units. So one can also speak of a popular Church in this sense, to denote the sort of authority being adopted by the ecclesiastical institution in order to link up its basic communities. Just as the Church once adopted a bureaucratic type of power structure—in which the constituted authority exercised power by attributing functions, legally defined, to hierarchically organised functionaries, whose person was separate from their office, as Max Weber has defined it[15]—so now it is trying out a form of community power structure, one that fits better with the experience people have in the other basic organisations in their lives.

This analysis leads us to conclude that from the sociological viewpoint it is possible to justify the use of the term 'popular Church' (*Igreja 'popular'*) to describe the form the ecclesiastical institution is taking as a result of its insertion in the popular movement, at least in the term 'people' (*i povo*), its meaning is being defined by the people themselves regardless of academic restrictions on its use. The expression 'popular Church' refers to a form, a style, a way of being Church which is the expression of the active participation of the people in it. In this first sense, one can speak of a popular Church just as one can speak of popular art, medicine or culture. But beyond this, the expression is justified to indicate the difference between this form of being Church, born of its insertion in the popular movement, and the bourgeois form, born of the Church's insertion in bourgeois society. A new phenomenon should be designated by a new expression. And this is, in the end, what justifies the use of the expression 'popular Church' in sociology.

Translated by Paul Burns

Notes

1. E.g. E. E. Evans-Pritchard *Social Anthopology* (London n/d).
2. Cicero *De Republica* 25.
3. D. Azambuja *Teoria geral do Estado* (Porto Alegre 1971) p. 19. see also L. Sánchez Agesta *Princípios de teoría política* (Madrid 1976) p. 132.
4. See L. Salaverri SJ 'Ecclesia societas perfecta', thesis 23, nn. 937–971 in *Sacrae Theologiae Summa* (Madrid 1958).
5. N. Werneck Sodré *Introduçao à revoluçao brasiliera* (Rio de Janeiro 1963) p. 188.
6. See O. Ianni *A formaçao do Estado populista na América Latina* (Rio de Janeiro 1975) p. 14.
7. See C. Mendes *Nacionalismo e desenvolvimento* (Rio de Janeiro 1963) pp. 15–16.
8. Besides the works mentioned in notes 5, 6 and 7 above, see also: H. Jaguaribe *O nacionalismo na atualidade brasiliera* (Rio de Janeiro 1958) Part I; O. Ianni *O colapso do populismo no Brasil* (Rio de Janeiro 1968).
9. See Ianni, the work cited in note 6, chs. 1, 2, 12.
10. I have taken for analysis the accounts prepared by the Basic Communities for the third Inter-ecclesial Meeting in 1978. Although these texts were all prepared by Catholics, they can be taken as representative of popular thinking in general, since they contain contributions from both urban and rural communities spread over the whole of Brazil—a total of 22 documents, of which eight refer to several communities. Reading them, I noted all the times the words 'people' ('*povo*') or 'popular' ('*popular*') appeared, analysing the sense in which they were being used. The accounts were published in *SEDOC* III, 115, Oct. 1978.
11. See E. Wanderley 'Comunidades eclesiais de base e educaçao popular' in *Rev. Ecles. Bras.*, 41, 164 (Dec. 1981) pp. 686–707. See also L. A. Gomez de Souza *Classes populares e Igreja nos caminhos da història* (Petròpolis 1982), Part 3.
12. There is a fine example of this in the account made by the team of theologians in the Latin-American Confederation of Religious in CLAR, *Povo de Deus e comunidade libertadora* (Rio de Janeiro 1979), esp. pp. 35–70. It is in this context that the opposition between 'people-class' ('*povo-*

classe') (see e.g. F. Castillo 'Christianity: bourgeois religion or religion of the people?' in *Concilium* 125) and 'people-nation' ('*povo-nacao*') (see e.g. J. Scannone *Teología de la liberación y praxis popular* (Salamanca 1976) pp. 69–70.

13. See P. Ribeiro de Oliveira 'Oprimidos: a opção pela Igreja' *Rev. Ecles. Bras.*, 41, 164 (Dec. 1981) 643–653.

14. See *Concilium* 125 on 'Christianity and the Bourgeoisie', esp. the articles by Castillo (cited in note 12) and J.-B. Metz) 'Messianic or bourgeois religion? On the crisis of the Church in West Germany'.

14. See M. Weber *Economie et société* I, (Paris 1971) pp. 223–227. For a commentary on the concept of bureaucracy, see R. Bendix *Max Weber: an Intellectual Portrait* (London 1966) pp. 423–430.

Leonardo Boff

A Theological Examination of the Terms 'People of God' and 'Popular Church'

IN THEOLOGICAL terms, the expression 'People of God' is as ambiguous as Pedro Ribeiro de Oliveira has shown it to be in sociological terms. As it is a historical concept, its meaning depends on its historico-religious contexts, which must be studied separately. Specific historical situations yield five meanings for the term, and a sixth is being worked out within the phenomenon that is our concern throughout this article, the Church of the Poor, or 'Popular Church' (*Igreja dos pobros ou a Igreja Popular*). My theological purpose here will be to show how far the sociological reality of the popular Church, which Ribeiro de Oliveira has shown to exist as a sociological reality, can be taken as a possible embodiment of the theological reality of the People of God. This would give a new meaning to the latter term. On one hand, an existing meaning of 'people of God' would find its historical embodiment in the popular Church; on the other, this historical embodiment would serve to enrich the traditional understanding of the People of God.

It is important not to lose sight of the phenomenon that posed such a challenge to ecclesiological thinking: the emergence of the popular Church (*Igreja Popular*).[1] A mass of people without consciousness of their situation, without their own historical purpose and lacking adequate means, under the influence of a number of factors, began to organise themselves into communities and associations of all sorts, in other words, into popular movements. In process terms, *the mass became a people*, that is, an organised entity taking stock of itself and working out a social practice with a view to their partication in society and the transformation of that society. Church bodies—bishops, priests, pastoral workers—took part in this more general mobilisation from a more specifically religious standpoint. As the majority of the people are poor and mainly Christian, there arose ecclesial communities in their districts, and these produced lay pastoral workers, prayer groups and action groups. Important sectors of the institutional Church supported this process and made themselves part of the people's progress: the Church became a people's Church (*a Igreja se faz popular*). The people took part in the life of the Church, created popular expressions of faith and felt themselves to be the Church; the Christian people defined themselves as the People of God. Such a phenomenon involved a new way of being the Church,[2] built around the axis of the community and the participation of everyone, which in turn forced the various ranks in the Church, from cardinal to lay person, to re-define themselves. In place of a Church-society with centralised and hierarchical authority, with anonymous and functional relationships, there began to be a communion-

and-community Church with a more equitable distribution of sacred authority, with organic and more participatory relationships.

This ecclesial reality, which calls itself the 'all-brothers Church' (*Igreja-todos-irmãos*) or 'all-People-of-God Church (*Igreja-todos-Povo-de-Deus*) (and it includes cardinals, bishops, priests, religious, theologians, lay organisers and simple militant faithful working in basic communities or even in trade unions with a clear Christian purpose)—what is it? Can it be called, in all theological strictness, really and not metaphorically, the People of God? And what, in the end, do we mean by 'People of God'?

1. THE MEANINGS OF 'PEOPLE OF GOD' AND THEIR HISTORICAL CONTEXTS

Let us consider the main meanings of the term 'People of God', as they were worked out theologically from the background of particular historico-religious situations.[3]

(a) Israel as People of God

According to the constant theology of the Old Testament, Israel saw itself as the people chosen by Yahweh, the people of the alliance, placed in the midst of other peoples with the mission of showing them the true God, being a mediator of salvation for them and enabling all peoples to become the People of God.[4] A critical theology which takes account of the historical character of revelation will try to identify the specific mediations—the material and ideological bases—which made this revelation possible.[5] In a word: for Israel to be the People of God (theology) it was first necessary for it to be a people (history). It is therefore important to link sociology with theology in such a way as to avoid mystification (the divine explanation of social realities) and theologism (the religious factor explains everything) as much as sociologism (sociological explanations are the only valid ones for religious experience). So an attentive consideration of the economic, social, political, military and religious factors (which there is no space for here) will lead to an understanding of the process by which the children of Israel (Bene-Israel) formed themselves into a people which later, under the monarchy, gave itself a State.[6] Within this process of constitution of a people there was also the consciousness of the event of the revelation of an election, an alliance, of promises and of the mission entrusted to them by Yahweh, so that this people understood itself to be the People of God.

Briefly, the process went like this: the clans (Patriarchs) and tribes were reduced in Egypt to subjugated masses. One group that had Yahweh as its God-protector managed to organise itself and escaped spectacularly, taking others with it; in order to keep its political-military hegemony it imposed its religion, obtained sufficient internal cohesion to dislodge the previous settlers in Canaan and aggregate other tribes to itself. Israel emerged as a people from the moment when the various tribes established a federation among themselves so as to be able to undertake wars of liberation against neighbours militarily and culturally stronger than themselves. Under the invocation of Yahweh-Sabaoth (Josh. 24), a covenant was made among the tribes. The motive for this was the need for subsistence (material base); the cohesive element was religious (theological fact: Josh. 24:21–24). The union of these two factors meant that such religious-political force was generated that Israel prevailed over all its neighbours.

That is a very summary account of the constitution of the people of Israel, who had a clear understanding of themselves, a defined political-religious objective and adequate organisation. This fact provides the material basis for the emergence of the People of God. Just as the people had chosen their God, now in their religious experience they felt chosen by God gratuitously; just as a covenant had been made among all the people at Schechem (Josh. 25:25), so they felt that God was making a covenant with his people. The formula became classical and resounds throughout the whole of the Old Testament: 'I shall be your God, and you will be my people' (Exod. 6:7; Lev. 26:12; Deut. 26: 17; 2 Sam. 7:24; Jer. 7:23; Ezek. 11:20). The people became the People of God either because they chose God or because they were chosen by God. Chronologically, the people came before the People of God. Theologically, the People of God comes first in God's purpose and it was as a support for this privilege that the historical framework of a people was formed. The people only became fully a people when they expressed their inner dynamic in the direction of God and thereby became the People of God. Israel appears as a sacrament of that which can and should happen to all peoples: they will be Peoples of God (Rev. 21:3).

(b) The Church of the New Testament as the true and new People of God

The early Christian community saw itself initially not as the new People of God, but as the *true* and faithful People of God. Through their acceptance of Jesus and the new relationship he had inaugurated with God (new covenant), they saw the promises of the Old Testament fully realised in themselves.[7] By calling themselves *ecclesia*, a translation of the Septuagint's term *kahal* for the People of God, and by stressing the importance of the twelve as a symbolic number representing the twelve tribes, they demonstrated the continuity of the same divine calling and mission. They formed themselves into communities, with a clear consciousness of their Christian identity (the Nazarene sect, '*hairesis*', Acts 22:5; 28:22). They formed a little people and a People of God (*um povo pequeno e um Povo de Deus*), both marked by Judaic culture.

The *new* People of God (*o novo Povo de Deus*) stemmed from the missionary activity of Paul. These were the Gentiles who formed Christian communities directly, without the mediation of Judaism. Through faith and conversion to Christ, other peoples could become Peoples of God (*Povos de Deus*), as Luke stresses in his account of Pentecost: 'We hear them preaching in our own language about the marvels of God' (Acts 2:11). James told the council of Jerusalem, 'how God first visited the Gentiles, to take out of them a people for his name' (15:14). The new People of God was made up of the union and communion of a vast network of Christian communities spread throughout various peoples. The material basis for this People of God was not made up of a common culture, language, origin and destiny, as with the Jewish people; the support was the local community, with its own insertion in the culture of its environment, its own Christian consciousness and practices, as is clear from the letters of Paul and Christian literature of the first two centuries. The term 'new People of God', expressing the sum total of individual churches (domestic, urban, rural, provincial communities), acquired a spiritual dimension through the strength of its all-embracing extent. We should not be surprised if even in Apostolic times there was a tendency to deny the continuity of this new People of God with the People of God of the Old Testament.[8] The latter was seen as the prototype of infidelity and sin. Continuity came to be seen no longer in historic-salvific terms, but in metaphysical ones. From the time the basic support-group, the *communities*, started to disappear, giving place to a Church of Christian masses, with no effective participation, the concept of People of God faded away till it ended up as a metaphorical understanding, divorced from history and limited to formal theological categories: the sum total of all the baptised in the visible unity of the Church; the effective participation of the faithful in the production of the Church and its services was no longer required as a condition for safeguarding the minimum content of the concept.

(c) Christendom as the realisation of the political concept of the People of God

As Christianity spread through other cultures and became the dominant religious ideology of society, many of the Fathers began to confer a political meaning on the notion of People of God. They called Christians a special people—*tertium genus*, apart from Gentiles and Jews.[9] Just as the *populus romanus* formed a political entity embracing far-flung racial and geographical groups, the same happened to the Christian people: it became a people formed out of all peoples (*um povo formado de todos os povos*) as soon as they became part of the Christian ethos (faith, dress, worship, culture), they were guaranteed their character as People of God. Augustine spoke of the *ecclesia omnium gentium*.[10] This concept reached its apogee when the regime of Christendom was effectively installed: the occupation of all geographical and cultural space by Christianity, producing a society ideologically and also politically led by the hierarchy of the Church working with the secular rulers.[11] The *populus tuus* of the liturgical texts referred to the faithful gathered to worship, but its historical presupposition was the regime of Christendom, in which the faithful were hegemonised by the hierarchy within a clerical framework.

(d) The People of God as 'simple faithful'

This conception of the People of God, while maintaining its universal character, in fact tends to accentuate the importance of the clergy, to the extent of making them simply synonymous with the Church, the community of the ordained, bearers of sacramental power and possessors of all the means of religious production. 'People of God' then becomes synonymous with lay people, a sense already found in the Latin Fathers, such as Tertullian, Cyprian and Optatus of Milan. The lay People of God, according to Gratian, 'has the duty to submit itself to the clergy, to obey them, to carry out their orders and to render them honour'.[12] Analytically, the People of God here becomes the mass of the faithful who attend church, excluded from any power of decision-making in the institutional Church. It supposes an unequal constitution of the Church which forces one to interpret terms of ecclesial inter-relationship such as brotherhood and community in a spiritual sense.

(e) The whole Church, clergy and laity, makes up the messianic People of God

The second Vatican Council tried to overcome the view of two sorts of Christian. After emphasising the mystery/sacrament character of the Church, it sought to introduce a concept that would embrace all the faithful before any internal distinctions were made.[13] It chose the term 'People of God' to express this; in doing so it recovered the biblical dimension of history, covenant, election, consecration/mission and pilgrimage en route to the eschatological Kingdom. It underlined the mutual ordination of the ministerial priesthood and the general priesthood, meeting in the one priesthood of christ (LG 10). This messianic People is sent out into the whole world, since the whole human race is in some way called to it (LG 9; 13). While the messianic People of God is made up of the members of the Church in the full sense, others—members of other Christian bodies and other religions, and even atheists of good will who lead a virtuous life—are also related to it in various ways.[14] The People of God can be understood as the sum total of all the justified, though with different degrees of insertion in the reality of the Church (LG 14–16). The idea is that redeemed humanity, which receives grace through a just life, makes up the greater People of God, loved by God and created for a happy destiny in the eschatological Kingdom.[15] Within this greater People, the messianic People of God, which is the Church in its historical institutional embodiment, emerges with a sacramental function of sign and instrument.

The whole of Vatican II's concept of the People of God is shot through with the need for the participation and communion of all the faithful in the prophetic, priestly and royal service of Christ (LG 10–12), which means their active insertion in the various ecclesial services, in the charisms given for the common good (LG 12). This People of God is actualised in individual Churches and in particular cultures whose values and customs are adopted and purified (LG 13). While there are distinctions, 'yet all share a true equality with regard to the dignity and activity common to all the faithful for the building up of the Body of Christ' (LG 32).

For Vatican II the People of God only comes into existence when communities have a historical existence, the fruit of the incarnation of faith in the midst of the characteristics of each people. This is not a formal concept devoid of historical materiality. It seeks to be a real and not metaphorical designation of the Church; but for it to be a real designation there has to be the real historical existence of a people which through its manner of organising itself in its Christian faith emerges as the People of God.

2. THE HISTORICAL-SOCIAL CONTENT OF THE PEOPLE OF GOD

The preceding account shows the need to make some distinctions. In any entity that is called People of God, there has to be a real People of God, in a historical, not analogical or metaphorical sense. This and Ribeiro de Oliveira's analysis clearly show that *in order to speak properly of a people or of a People of God* (povo e também de Povo de Deus) *there has to be conscious participation and communitary organisation around a project.* In the case of the People of God, *Lumen Gentium* emphatically states: 'Its goal is the Kingdom of God, which has been begun by God himself on earth, and which is to be extended until it is brought to perfection by Him at the end of time' (LG 9).

Analytically, neither people nor People of God are a *fact* but an *event*; they result from a process of communitary productive forces. In the first place there is an oppressed or dispersed mass; this in the non-people (see Hos. 1:6, 9; 1 Pet. 2:10) seeking to become a people. 'People' here describes not a *datum* but a *desideratum*, a protest against massification and a damand for a value to which all can have access: being able to participate in and be subjects of their own history; when the Christian masses call themselves people or People of God, they are expressing demand long denied to them by discriminatory élites who destroy the channels of participation. The mass begins to produce active factors (charismatic leaders, resistance groups determined on survival) which give origin to communities. These in turn work on the mass, helping it to take stock of itself and to work in terms of a project to be carried out. Then the articulation of communities (associations, groups, movements, etc.) among themselves plus their activity together with and in the midst of the mass makes a people emerge. If this people is to hold together, it needs to solidify its means of participation and to keep a sharp watch on its power structures so that individuals are not returned to the mass with the character of people taken away from them.

A Church in which lay people cannot participate in sacred authority, in which decisions are concentrated within the clerical body, cannot really call itself the People of God; it lacks the communion and participation expressed by communities and groups that live their faith with relative autonomy. Unlike a People of God, there will be a mass of faithful, frequenting some chapel or parish church, alongside a hierarchy which retains control over word, sacrament and the conduct of the faithful. Subject lay people and the mass of the faithful in a regime of Christendom do not, analytically, constitute the People of God, though they may have been called such at times in history. For the Church to become the People of God (*Para que a Igreja se torne Povo de Deus*) it must, primarily, *bring into focus those characteristics that form a people: consciousness, community and practices designed to enhance consciousness and the possibilities of participation and communion within the community.* This people becomes a people *of God* when it allows itself to be evangelised, when it comes together around the Word of God forming Christian communities and organises a practice inspired by the gospel and the proper living Tradition of the Church. Without this historical-social content one cannot properly speak of Church-People-of-God. The situation of the faithful being merged in Christ through faith or baptism is better defined by the expression. Church-body-of-Christ.[16] But it is important to point out that the proper theological nature of faith, of baptism and of the body-of-Christ carries a historical-social intentionality; they all essentially require expression in communities in which there is participation and the experience of evangelical brotherhood (see LG 8).

3. THE POPULAR CHURCH AS A HISTORICAL EMBODIMENT OF THE PEOPLE OF GOD

The popular Church (*A Igreja Popular*) of Latin America, as briefly described in the first section, grew up as a result of renewal in the Church inspired by Vatican II.[17] The second chapter of *Lumen Gentium*, dealing with the People of God, was taken seriously; lay people felt encouraged to play their part at all levels in the Church; bishops responded to the call to be more pastors, part of the march of the faithful, than ecclesiastical authorities set apart from challenges arising from social factors, particularly those facing the immense majority of the poor.

Lumen Gentium's proposal that the whole Church should become the pilgrim People of God was at once a challenge and a command; it did not correspond to any existing embodiment of the Church, and could not be brought into being without profound changes. These had to be put into effect and *are still being worked out*. The model of the Church as a perfect society under the hegemony of the clergy, leading to the pathology of clericalism, is giving way more and more to Church as communications network structured round the participation of everyone, producing a true People of God. The concept of a People of God built on this base is one of its possible historical embodiments, without excluding different ones in other contexts. Let us consider some of the characteristics of this expression of the People of God.[18]

(a) The sociologically popular character of the Church

The popular Church is made up predominantly, though not exclusively, of people who formerly belonged to the vast marginalised masses of society, who organised themselves into popular movements; in the church sphere, they were the scattered, badly-served faithful, who then formed a vast network of communities and prayer and action groups. Large numbers of people from the institutional ranks of the Church, bishops, priests and religious, went along with these people and church groups, forming the whole that we call the popular Church. It is called popular because the people (in the sociological sense) hold the potential power to lead the process. Taking part in any manifestation of the popular Church is enough to make one realise the massive presence of the people, generally poor and of mixed race. Christian faith has taken flesh in popular culture, characterised more by symbols than by concepts, more by narrative than by discourse, with a strong feeling for celebration, solidarity, the unity between gospel and life, the mysticism of everyday life, the dramatisation of the mysteries of faith. Those bishops and pastoral workers who became part of this process of the people becoming the People of God through faith experienced in community have adopted this popular version of the Church. They themselves have dispensed with the titles and trappings that distanced them from the people. Under the creative hegemony of the people, the style of the hierarchy's presence has changed, without renouncing its indispensable function of inspiration and unification; in the same way role of religious and theologians has changed into that of people who draw from the expressions of popular faith and who think their faith in conjunction with the experiences and challenges of the community.

(b) **The popular Church and the Church of the poor** *(A Igreja Popular é a Igreja dos pobros)*

Statistically, most of the members of the popular Church are poor. In this type of Church, the paternalistic relationship with the poor, which allowed no room for making use of the social and ecclesial strength of the poor, has been largely overcome; now the poor participate within a framework that they have worked out for themselves. Those who are not poor have taken on the cause of the poor in the popular Church and made the 'preferential option' that the whole Church is supposed to have taken for the poor something true and effective. Therefore they too truly belong to the Church of the poor.

(c) **A Church fighting for liberation**

What the people and the poor seek above all is to escape from the poverty that prevents them from living. They see poverty as a social injustice contrary to God's purpose. The popular Church sees as self-evident that the integral liberation willed by God requires an equitable sharing of goods (see Acts 2:44; 4:32–34); poverty as well as riches have to be set aside in the quest for just and fraternal relations. This process means carrying on the struggle through evangelical means, but it has nevertheless produced assassinations and real martyrdoms perpetrated by those (many of them Christians) who do not wish to see anything changed so as to hold on to their privileges. Phrases current among Christian militants are: 'I am a fighter for the Gospel'; 'I am in the fight for the liberation of my brothers'.

(d) **A Church on the way** *(uma Igreja du cominhada)*

This is a key phrase in this type of Church, meaning basically: there is a profound shift of the Church from the centre to the periphery, involving a clerical Church changing itself into a popular Church; it also means that the formation of a popular Church is a never-finished process, something dynamic, always open to connections between Gospel and life and disposed to welcome all those who wish to live their faith in community. So it is said: 'Such-and-such a bishop has set out on the way'.

(e) **A Church of and from the base**

Among the various meanings of 'base', two stand out here: the base as the organised people; not only members (lay) of the people make up the popular Church; it also includes the various religious authorities such as bishops, priests, religious and pastoral workers; all these have gone back to the base and set out on the way. 'Base' is also a political-ecclesiastical concept; a distinction is drawn between the human source of power (base: the organised people) and the exercise of power (apex: the sacred ministries). The exercise of authority in the popular Church is carried out with constant reference to the bases; questions are discussed and responses worked out in the bases, which always include those who exercise authority. Consensus and communion are worked out from the base, in such a way that authoritarian crystallisations of power can never come about.

(f) **A Church of political holiness**

Through its dependence on the base and its popular character, the popular Church is constantly in conflict with society, faced with problems of poverty, injustice and violence, problems primarily political in nature. In seeking liberation from social injustice, Christians, besides exercising the personal virtues, which are always important, must necessarily evolve a political holiness: loving within the class struggle, hoping for results that can only come in a far-off future, taking the part of the oppressed, ascetically obeying decisions taken by the community and, ultimately, being prepared to lay down their lives for the sake of the Gospel and their oppressed brethren.

(g) A Church open to everyone

The popular Church, by the very fact of being popular, is not a ghetto, nor a parallel Church. All those who decide to live the Gospel and to follow Jesus by associating themselves with the struggles of the great majority, will find a joyful welcome in it. This type of Church offers a challenge of conversion to the whole Church—from the style in which the papacy is exercised to the way in which faith and life are combined in every life-situation.

4. CONCLUSION: FULFILLING THE DIVINE WILL TO FOUND A CHURCH

The popular Church, as it is taking shape, not only embodies the theological concept of the People of God, especially as elaborated by Vatican II, but enriches it in so far as it allows the people, in the sociological sense, poor and Christian people, to take on the role of hegemony in forming the ecclesial community. In doing so, it does not exclude the hierarchy, but incorporates it in love; changed in style and given a place, it too belongs to the popular Church. Because of this, there is obviously no reason why there should be any opposition, on principle, between the hierarchy and the popular Church. There is a certain tension, and sometimes opposition, between a type of Church that prolongs its incarnation in the ruling bourgeois culture, with the interests vested in this, and this new type of Church which is taking flesh in the popular culture, changing, championing the cause of the people and therefore, rightly, calling itself a popular Church.[19] The interests of the organised people do not always coincide with, and indeed are often opposed to, those who do not want to share the people's cause, preferring to live at the expense of the people. As there are Christians on both sides, one can understand the conflicts that can arise, primarily social in character and ecclesial only at second hand.

The emergence of the popular Church from within a 'Christendom-style' Church with too great a separation between clergy and faithful, between rich Christians and poor, all of whom are now brought together in a community with participation at all levels, built from the bottom up but open to all directions, seeking justice and liberty for all, fulfils the permanent will of Christ and his Spirit to found a Church that would be an assembly of all peoples on their way to the final Kingdom.

Translated by Paul Burns

Notes

1. See the essays collected in *Una Iglesia que nace del pueblo* (Salamanca 1979).

2. Document produced by the Brazilian National Bishops' Conference on Basic Ecclesial Communities (São Paulo 1983), n. 3.

3. The most important overall views of the question are: M. Keller *'Volk Gottes' als Kirchenbegriff* (Einsiedeln 1970); Y. Congar 'The Church: the People of God', in *Concilium* 1 (1965); R. Schnackenburg and J. Dupont 'The Church as the People of God' in *ibid.*; O. Semmelroth 'The People of God' in *The Church of Vatican II* ed. J. Baraúna (London and New York 1965).

4. The basic works are: N. A. *Dahl Das Volk Gottes* (Darmstad 1963); A. Oepke *Das neue*

Gottesvolk in Schriftum, bildender Kunst und Weltgestaltung (Guterslöh 1950); H. H. Rowley *The Biblical Doctrine of Election* (London 1950).

5. Important on this point are: A. Causse *Du Groupe ethnique à la communauté religieuse: le problème sociologique de la Religion d'Israel* (Paris 1937); J. Pirenne *La Société hebraïque* (Paris 1965); M. Weber *Le Judaïsme antique* (Paris 1970).

6. See C. Boff *La Formation du peuple d'Israel* (Louvain 1973, dupl.)

7. J. Jocz *A Theory of Election, Israel and the Church* (London 1958); W. Trilling 'Das wahre Israel' in *Studien zur Theologie des Matthäusevangeliums* (Leipzig 1959).

8. See the texts in Keller *'Volk Gottes'*, the work cited in note 3, pp. 17–25.

9. See the texts in M. Simon *Versus Israel* (Paris 1948) pp. 135ff.

10. *In Ps. 47, 2*, PL 36, 533; *In Ps. 56,13*, PL 36, 669f.

11. The most perinent study is that of P. Richard *Morte das cristandades e nascimento da Igreja* (São Paulo 1982).

12. *Decretal of Gratian* Ch. 7, c. XII, q. 1(Friedberg I, 679); other similar texts can be found in Y. Congar *Lay People in the Church* (London 1957).

13. See A. Acerbi *Due Ecclesiologie* (Bologna 1975) pp. 345–61, 508–26; H. Hostein *Hiérarchie et Peuple de Dieu d'après Lumen Gentium* (Paris 1970).

14. See L. Boff *Die Kirche als Sakrament in Horizont der Welterfahrung* (Paderborn 1972) pp. 399–441.

15. See K. Rahner 'People of God' in *Sacramentum Mundi* IV pp. 400–402.

16. For the relationship between Church as People of God and the mystical body of Christ, see M. Schmaus *Katholische Dogmatik* III/1 (Munich 1958) pp. 204–230.

17. The more significant titles are: J. B. Libanio 'Igreja que nasce da religião do povo' in Var. *Religião e Catolicismo do povo* (Curitiba 1977), pp. 119–175; P. Suess *Catholicismo popular no Brasil* (São Paulo 1979); R. Munoz *La Iglesia en el pueblo; hacia una eclesiologia latinoamericana* (Santander 1981); J. Sobrino *Resurrectión de la verdadera Iglesia* (Santander 1981); T. Ellacuria 'Pueblo de Dios' in *Conceptos fundamentales de Pastoral* (Madrid 1983) pp. 840–859; G. Casalis ' "Pueblo de Dios": experiencias históricas, utopia movilizadora' in Var. *La esperanza en el presente de América Latina* (San José de Costa Rica 1983) pp. 409–419; H. E. Groenen 'Na Igreja, quem é o povo?' in *Rev Ecles. Bras.* 39 (1979) 195–221.

18. There is a fuller account in L.Boff *Igreja: carisma e poder* (Petrópolis 1981) pp. 172–195.

19. See F. Castillo 'Christianity: Bourgeois Religion or Religion of the People?' in *Concilium* 125 (1979) 51–60.

Edward Schillebeeckx

Offices in the Church of the Poor

1. THE CHURCH AS THE PEOPLE OF GOD:
'THE COMMUNITY OF GOD'

A great deal has happened in the Church and its many different forms since the appearance of the French original of Yves Congar's *Lay People in the Church* in 1953.[1] The author's purpose when he wrote this book was to break through the then current practice of equating the Church with the hierarchy. Some of the basic ideas contained in his book found their way into the final edition of the Dogmatic Constitution on the Church, *Lumen Gentium*, of Vatican II. A whole chapter on the people of God, the Church, was inserted into that document even before the question of offices was mentioned in that context. In it, the Church—the people of God—was called 'priestly, pastoral and prophetic' and was seen as sharing as a whole in the threefold ministry of Jesus as the Christ. The 'community of Christ' is therefore, as the community joined to Jesus, the leader of the 'messianic people' who are filled with the Spirit, itself the subject of prophetic, pastoral and priestly activity, whereas offices are within this whole—and presupposing this priestly substance of the people of God—a diaconal or 'ministerial' concentration of what is common to all believers. They are a ministry for the benefit of that priestly people of God, the Church. As derived from the priestly character of Jesus Christ and his messianic community, the Roman Catholic Church was also eventually not wrong to call the official ministries for the benefit of the priestly community of Christ 'prophetic, pastoral and priestly'. This was, however, a one-sided development, even though it was historically and theologically quite legitimate.

Before, during and for some time after the Second Vatican Council, there was a great deal of discussion about a 'theology of the laity'. On closer inspection, however, it emerged that many forms of that theology of the laity were unconsciously based on the same 'hierarchical' premises. Attempts were made to give the concept 'laity', which was still seen as 'non-clergy', a positive content and the fact that this positive content had already been provided by the Christian meaning of the word *christifidelis* was often overlooked. The distinctive aspect of the lay person was defined as his (or her) relationship with the world. That of the member of the clergy was seen as his relationship with the Church. This meant that both the ecclesial dimension of the the *christifidelis* and his relationship with the world were distorted. The member of the clergy thus became the 'a-political man of the Church', while the layman became the 'politically committed' man of the world who was hardly committed at all to the Church. The ontological status of the 'new man' who had been reborn through baptism in the Spirit was therefore, according to this view, not recognised in his (or her) own distinctive value, but only seen from the point of view of the status of the clergy. But that is not a status at all, but a ministry for the service or benefit of the Church, a 'church-functional' ministry. The 'ontological' status obtained through baptism in the Spirit was therefore misinterpreted, whereas the office was raised to the level of a status with serious ontological connotations.

The mediaeval concept 'non-clergy', layman, continued to have an influence here. The 'lay person' was equated with the 'idiota', the uneducated, poor and carnal man, *vir saecularis*, the man of the world (because no thought was given either in the Church or in society to women at that time). Apart from such 'powerful laymen' as emperors and princes, who were in any case hardly regarded as 'laymen' and were indeed sacrally anointed, laymen were above all stupid and obedient people, subjected to the *maiores*, the educated. This social situation also had a theological substructure. Jurists and even theologians divided the Church community into two genera, *ordines* or statuses: the *ordo clericorum* (to which the *ordo monachorum* was to some extent assimilated) and the *ordo laicorum*. This division into orders or statuses also had serious social and even ethical implications: 'duo ordines, clericorum et laicorum; duae vitae, spiritualis et carnalis'[2] or, as this idea was expressed elsewhere: the basis of the Church consisted of 'carnal and married people' and the top of the Church of 'consecrated (celibate) clergy and religious'.[3]

I know that this has to be taken with a grain of salt. But it is true to say that this pyramidical hierarchical structure of the Church community, which was partly inspired by the social status symbols of the waning Graeco-Roman Empire, was powerfully influenced from the sixth century onwards by the neo-Platonic works of Pseudo-Dionysius.[4] Pastoral and sociological differences in the Church were given a theological infrastructure in the light of this neo-Platonic vision of the world and the various ministries in the Church were 'hierarchicised', that is, they became gradually descending realities of decreasing value. The higher level, in other words, came to possess in an eminent manner what the lower level possessed as poor-relief and limited power. The official functions of all the 'lower' ministries could be found in absolute fullness at the highest level, which had since time immemorial been, historically speaking, the episcopate. In this way, in accordance with an authentically neo-Platonic view of the world, all power came 'from above'.

This 'hierarchicisation' of the top of the Church, however, led to a devaluation of the laity at the base of the pyramid and lay people became simply objects of priestly pastoral care. In principle, the clergy, with the episcopate enjoying the highest *status perfectionis*, realised in a perfect manner a religious pattern of life and were in perfect union with God. Ordinary believers, on the other hand, could only experience and achieve that religious way of life and unity with God indirectly and imperfectly—in obedience to the *maiores*. It has to be said quite bluntly that this neo-Platonic hierarchical view of the Church is nowadays quite untenable. It is also diametrically opposed to the New Testament vision of the Church.

2. THE NEW TESTAMENT VISION OF THE CHURCH AND ITS MINISTRIES

This in no way implies a form of biblicism, suggesting that we should nowadays try to imitate the undifferentiated forms of organisation in the early Church in the present-day organisation of the Church and its offices. It would be hermeneutically impossible to justify such a step. I therefore recognise in this case, on the one hand, the significance of the New Testament as a normative model and, on the other, the power of the rest of the history of the Church to inspire our present understanding of faith. I do not accept any form of biblicism, whether it points to the left or to the right. What I am concerned with is the historical mediation—the social and historical context that exists here and now in the world and the Church.

Men's experience of God's care for them as revealed in Jesus' message and way of life was the origin of the first wave of the Jesus movement, which was initiated above all by Hebrew-speaking (or Aramaic-speaking) Jews who had become Christians and who were waiting for the Lord Jesus to come to judge the world. In the New Testament, however, it was above all those sections of the early Christian Jesus movement consisting of Greek-speaking Jews in the Diaspora who had been converted to Christianity who were given a hearing. It was among them that the Judaeo-Christian movement became a Church with a universal mission. Their faith, the structure of their Church and their mission were not directly based on experience of the historical Jesus (whom they had never met). These were based rather on their baptism in the Spirit (later called 'baptism and confirmation')—their baptism 'in the name of Jesus', also known as baptism-anointing. The God of those Christians was (and is) the God who did not abandon Jesus, but made him a 'life-giving spirit' (1 Cor. 15:45b). Christians who were baptised in him were therefore *pneumatici*—men and women who were 'filled with the Spirit', even though this prophetic power of the Spirit was manifested more in one Christian than in another and differently in different Christians. That is why it was said by members of the second or third generation of Christians that the Church was 'built upon the foundation of the apostles and prophets' (Eph. 2:20; 4:7–16) and why Paul was able to speak within the one brotherhood of many different charisms.

That community of faith was an 'egalitarian' brotherhood and sisterhood, a *koinonia*, assembly and coming together of partners who had been made equal in and through the Spirit:

> For in Christ Jesus you are all sons of God ...
> For as many of you as were baptised into Chtist
> have put on Christ.
> There is neither Jew nor Greek,
> there is neither slave nor free,
> there is neither male nor female;
> for you are all one in Christ Jesus

(Gal. 3:26–28)

This passage is a pre-Pauline baptismal tradition—a solemn declaration made over newly baptised Christians. As there is now a fairly universal consensus of opinion regarding this among exegetes, there is no need for me to justify my use of it here.[5] This baptismal tradition moreover goes back to the early Christian *pneuma* Christology and ecclesiology. The linguistically striking expression 'there is neither male nor female' (not, it should be noted, 'there is neither man nor woman') is an implicit reference to the Septuagint translation of Gen. 1:27 ('male and female he created man'). According to this way of thinking, Christian baptism in the Spirit is the eschatological restoration of an order of creation of equality and solidarity that was at that time (and is still today) experienced both historically and socially as disturbed: 'a new creation' (Gal. 6:15).

Baptism in the Spirit, then, does away with historical and social discriminations and inequalities. The victims of discrimination mentioned in this passage are, first, the heathens (discriminated against in favour of the Jews), secondly, slaves (discriminated against in favour of free men) and, thirdly, women (discriminated against in favour of men). (This Judaeo-Christian list could easily be extended nowadays.)

All historical and social antitheses are done away with in principle by Christian baptism and initially in the Christian community of faith itself. Baptismally, this is, of course, a performative, not a descriptive way of speaking, in other words, a way of speaking that expresses the hope of the Christian community, a hope that has to become a reality in that community of God as an example of how to live together. There should be no relationships of subjection between 'master' and 'subject' and no forms of discrimination within the Church at least. All three synoptics state very emphatically that the way in which authority is exerted in the world 'shall not be so among you' (Mark 10:42–43; Matt. 20:24–28; Luke 22:24–27).

The New Testament vision of 'offices in the Church' is therefore determined by this principle. The early Christian 'egalitarian' *pneuma* ecclesiology does not in any sense exclude authority and leadership from the Church, but it does exclude authority exerted 'in the manner of the world'.

Office or rather offices did not develop in the early Christian churches as has been said so often as the result of a historical change from charism to institution. On the contrary, they came about as the result of a change from the many charisms shared by all Christians to a specialised charism possessed by only a few. From the sociological and from the ecclesial point of view, this is a case of differentiation of system. The charism of the many different ministries, which had its origin in the very varied power of the baptism in the Spirit of all members of the Christian community living from the Spirit, gradually became not so much swallowed up by as certainly concentrated in a specifically ecclesial office, especially in the post-Pauline communities. It is in fact possible to say that the fullness of the original baptism in the Spirit gradually became fragmented—a distinction was made between 'baptism' and 'confirmation' and between 'baptism' and 'office'. This was an ecclesial differentiation of system and it was justified both sociologically and theologically. The early Church was, after all, looking for the most suitable structures for itself. We should not therefore project later church structures back into the New Testament in order to deprive the Church's office of every new possibility of adaptation in the present-day Church. What this development, which can be analysed both sociologically and theologically, can teach us, then, is that the 'ontological status' of baptism in the Spirit continues to be both the bearer and the matrix of the Church's office. These relationships should not be turned upside down.

Specialisation by a few (or, expressed in the language of the Church, the vocation of a few) in doing what is common to all is a reality that is taken for granted in every group, whether it is sociological or (in the case of the Church community) ecclesial. It is moreover clear from social and historical analyses that whenever there is no specialised concentration of what concerns all members of a group, only very little of what is common to all is achieved in the long run. Ambrosiaster, the anonymous patristic theologian, had precisely this intuition, when several centuries later he observed the difference between the still quite vague divisions in the structure of the early Christian community and the institutional offices that had been firmly established later according to a Church order that had been set up in the meantime.[6] The danger inherent in this kind of development, however legitimate it may have been, is that this charism concentrated in the Church's office may swallow up the Spirit active elsewhere in (and even outside) the Church and therefore 'quench the Spirit' (see 1 Thess. 5:19) in the community as a whole. The pneumatic and charismatic dimension of the *ecclesia* should not be derived from the official Church ('official' in both senses of the word). The latter is rooted in the baptism in the Spirit of all Christians who enter the 'apostolic community', the *christifideles*, and must be seen to be thus rooted. In the opposite case, believers are no longer subjects of faith and the expression of faith. They are, in a word, no longer subjects of the Church.

The term 'apostolicity' has been used in this context. It has at least four different aspects. The first is the fundamental apostolicity of the local communities as 'built upon the foundation of the apostles and prophets' (Eph. 2:20), who founded and inspired the first Christian communities. The second aspect is the apostolicity of the *id quod traditum est*, the *paratheke* or entrusted pledge, the apostolic tradition to which the New Testament as the original document belongs. The third is the apostolicity of the *ecclesiae* or communities of faith themselves, which were directly or indirectly brought into being by the apostles and prophets and normalised by what was 'handed down'. Part of this aspect is the communities' obedience in faith to the Gospel and their consistent *praxis* of the Kingdom of God—what is known as the *sequela Jesu* or following Jesus. Finally, there is a fourth aspect: the apostolicity of the Church's offices in the already established churches—the so-called 'apostolic succession'.

Apostolicity, then, is a concept which is rich in content and cannot be simply reduced to the fourth aspect, apostolic succession. There are many different factors in the growth and preservation of the traditional process of the Catholica. The visible Church communities came about as communities of men and women with a common destiny who had lived in the tradition of Israel and, within it, especially in the tradition of Jesus of Nazareth, confessed as the Christ, the Son of God and Lord. On the basis of this, these communities confessed the same faith (although they used different modes of expression), celebrated their shared destiny and finally let their conduct be governed by the guide-line of the praxis of the Kingdom of God, a kingdom of justice and love in which Jesus had preceded them and set the example.

There are therefore many traditional factors keeping the Church on the right course: the foundation of the communities by the apostles and prophets, the traditional content of faith, the confession of faith and especially the *regula fidei*, the praxis of believers and indeed the whole life of the many *ecclesiae*, including especially their baptism and the Eucharist, and finally specific official ministries of many different kinds, differentiated in confrontation with social and cultural contexts and contexts within the Church itself. In the faithful and living preservation of the original evangelical inspiration and orientation, offices are an important factor, but only one such factor. The four aspects of apostolicity are, moreover, and always have been in a state of constant interaction with each other.

'What you have heard from me before many witnesses entrust to faithful men who will be able to teach others also' (2 Tim. 2:2). At the deepest level, the *apostolicum* is the Christian confession of faith and the community of faith based on that confession. Office-bearers place the whole of their ministry at the service of that community. The gradual historical development by which the Church's office acquired a central and fundamental importance and the devaluation of baptism in the Spirit that accompanied this development were in the course of the Church's history to reveal all kinds of detrimental side-effects. This situation also led to the development of what was until recently the 'classical' pattern: first, of teaching (by the Church hierarchy), secondly, of explaining (by the Church's theologians) and thirdly, of obedience and listening (by the believers, known as the laity) to the Church's teaching (as explained by the theologians). Where in this classical pattern is the reality of the *christifidelis*? Believers are no longer seen in this paradigm, ecclesially at least, as subjects, but are reduced to the level of objects of priestly activity. An attempt was made during the Second Vatican Council to break through the ideology of this paradigm, but the very divergent views of the Church held by the bishops led in the end to a compromise solution.

The result of this development, which had already commenced in the later patristic period, was that all the charisms of the Spirit were concentrated in and sometimes even annexed by the specific office of the Church and then also narrowed down and embedded juridically in that office. What had in the New Testament been an official diaconate, a ministry and a serving love arising from the wealth of all believers and given to increase the wealth of all was then expressed in terms of power (*potestas*) and, what is more, of two categories of power: the power of ordination and the power of jurisdiction.

In its Dogmatic Constitution on the Church at least, the Second Vatican Council avoided as far as possible using the term *potestas* and spoke of *ministeria* and *munera* (although there was, theologically speaking, a rather ambiguous distinction between these two terms). In any case, in *Lumen Gentium*, office is seen as ministry within and for the Church in the world. To begin with, the Council broke through the medieval and later juridicism that surrounded the Church's offices by minimising the distinction between the power of ordination and that of jurisdiction and by shading their meaning at least by affirming that jurisdiction (which, from the point of view of the Church, is certainly concerned with the inner bond between the community and office) is fundamentally and essentially already given in its sacramental basis (the sacrament of ordination).

Nonetheless, Vatican II sometimes situated the 'representation of Christ' in and through the Church's office in the one holding office as a person and not formally in the act itself of the exercise of office[7] (as Thomas, who was more modest in his claims, had done). This clearly points to a surviving confusion between two levels: the ontological level of baptism in the Spirit, which makes us a 'new creation', and the church-functional level of office—a function, nonetheless on a real, sacramental basis. This second level presupposes the first and deeper level of baptism in the Spirit, precisely in order to be what it in fact is. Representation of Christ in the Church does not occur simply on the basis of office, which is only a typological, diaconal concentration and crystallisation of the universal charism of the Spirit or a specialisation at the church-functional level of the official ministers who have been called, given a mandate and sent by the Church and the Spirit dwelling in the Church. It goes without saying that this diaconal ministry has to be associated with a Christian ethos and spirituality of office—what may even be called a 'mysticism' of office. This is, after all, almost the only aspect of offices discussed in the New Testament. The mystical profundity of the apostolic ecclesial communities that 'live from the Spirit' should never be undermined or neutralised by contrasting it with a more intense mystification of office and the persons of those holding office.

There is, then, in the great tradition of the Catholica, a subtle distinction between baptism and office, between the universal priesthood of all believers and the official priesthood. This distinction is, however, tilted in favour of the baptism in the Spirit of all believers and not in the other direction. It is in baptism that Christians share ontologically in the threefold ministry of Jesus. Office, on the other hand, is a (sacramental) function or, as the Second Vatican Council calls it pleonastically and rather hesitantly in the Decree on the Priesthood (*Presbyterorum Ordinis*, 2) a 'ministerial function'. It is a ministerial specialisation, a typological representation of the same threefold ministry of Christ and the whole of his Church. The three characters (baptism and confirmation and the sacrament of ordination) have frequently been presented as an increasingly full and more intensive share in Jesus' threefold ministry, each one representing a hierarchically higher step. This view was not held in the Middle Ages, but theologians in the baroque period saw the matter in this light, forgetting that baptism (and confirmation) were at a completely different level from office—a much deeper level, baptism being the reality that bears the others up. For this reason, it is sometimes also the basis of what the Church (rather juridically and even in a kind of *Deus ex machina*) calls the *supplet Ecclesia*. It is also the basis of extraordinary ministry in exceptional circumstances.

This unsound mystification of office and those holding office in the Church was reinforced by certain statements made by the French *Ecole de spiritualité*. Despite many excellent pronouncements about office, John Eudes, for example, could say: 'The Son of God makes you (= priests) sharers in his quality as mediator between God and men, in his dignity as the sovereign judge of the world, in his name and ministry as the redeemer of the world and in many other excellences attributed to him'.[8] The reason for this extremely 'mystifying' elevation of office and those holding office (which is unknown in the writings of Augustine or Thomas Aquinas, for example) can be found in the fact that this school departed from the whole of Catholic tradition and saw Jesus' priesthood as directly based not on his humanity, but on his divinity. John Henry Newman protested against this view in the nineteenth century in connection with the less 'mystifying', but otherwise very similar views expressed by Cardinal Manning.[9] If, on the other hand, we do what Thomas, for example, did and see Jesus' priesthood as directly based on his humanity, the Church's priesthood is given a more modest significance, which is in no way less authentically Christian and sacramental. It is somewhere at this point that the crisis of the present-day priesthood is to be found.

3. OFFICES IN A SOCIAL AND HISTORICAL CONTEXT

This mystification of the priesthood, together with an undervaluation of the new way of being a Christian would seem to be the main reason why many believers are wary of approaching the question of offices in the Church from a social and historical point of view. We have, it is true, to speak not only in sociological language, but also in the language of religion and theology about the Church's offices. There is, however, often an unacceptable dualism in this case. What can be made sociologically and historically intelligible is distinguished by many believers and even separated from what is experienced, correctly, by the 'community of God' as God's call and grace. Such Christians react, when they are confronted with sociological and historical data concerning office, by saying: 'Good, but the Church's office is more than that. It is not simply a sociological or historical phenomenon'. This may, again correctly, be a protest against a reduction of office to a purely sociological reality, but it is equally possible to reduce office theologically by looking for the aspect of grace that is present in office alongside, above or behind its social and historical forms. In such cases, two separate aspects are recognised that can only be approached from different points of view and can only be discussed in two different language games (namely the language of science and that of faith). This is correct, but the next step is to project these two aspects (that have been separated in the abstract) as such, that is, to project them as conceptually separate on to the screen of reality and, what is more, to do this at one and the same level. The result of this is that they are considered together, thus creating the greatest possible difficulties. There is, after all, no revelatory surplus alongside or above the concrete forms of office. To believe this would be a form of supernaturalism or dualism.

In this matter, we are concerned with one and the same reality. The form of office that has developed historically and can be analysed sociologically is precisely what the believer experiences and what he expresses in the language of faith as a concrete form of the Church's response to God's grace—the form of a fortunate, a less fortunate or even a pastorally wrong response in the Church to God's grace and the signs of the times. This particular aspect cannot be interpreted sociologically or historically. Yet the dualism favoured by so many Christians results in an attempt to make the Church's office immune from socio-historical and historical criticism. This is unwise both from the ecclesial and from the pastoral point of view and it cannot be justified theologically.

This brings me to the concluding section of this article, in which I deal with office in the socio-historical context of a Church present among the poor, oppressed and suffering people. I have given this section the same title as the article itself:

4. OFFICES IN A CHURCH OF THE POOR

(a) The socio-historical context

Forms of theology of office and practices of that office in the Church never come about in a vacuum. There is the area of the *ecclesia* itself and there is also the socio-historical and the socio-political area of society in which the churches live and develop their offices. It often happens that many different offices come about in a conflict for competencies and in a complicated process of role formation within a group and therefore as part of differentiation of system and in the long run also as a later theological justification of historically acquired positions of authority. In the first century, for example, there was (in addition to a peaceful co-existence) conflict between the 'prophets' and the 'presbyters' and between the offices of men and those of women and later, until the fourth century, there was also conflict between presbyters and deacons. In the middle ages, there was conflict for competencies between those responsible for diocesan and parochial pastoral care and those responsible for abbatial pastoral care. Later still, there was conflict between monks who were priests and canons regular and finally conflict between the mendicants, whose pastoral care was supradiocesan and those whose pastoral work was traditional, diocesan and parochial. The same fluctuations appeared in the theology of office, that of the 'victors' in these conflicts eventually becoming the dominant theology. (I am unfortunately not able to go more deeply into this here.)[10] This process is still continuing today, when we are aware of role conflicts in the Church between the 'traditional priests' and the 'pastoral workers' who are not ordained but who are the ones who are really inspiring the Christian communities.

(b) The *Iglesia popular*

The 'people's Church' has, in the understanding of Latin American theologians, a special meaning that is frequently misinterpreted. On the other hand, however, the term can certainly give rise to such misunderstandings. In the first place, after the experience of Nazism and fascism in the West, we are all justifiably suspicious of anything that smacks of the 'people'—the *Volk*. This is, however, quite alien to the thinking of the liberation theologians of Latin America, although, in view of the world-wide significance and importance of their theology, it might perhaps be better for them to avoid using terms with unfavourable connotations (which are, it hardly needs to be said, not intended by the theologians themselves). I know from my own experience that language can easily give rise to emotional theological connotations. For the sake of the matter itself—the 'people's Church'—it might be advisable to review the use of language, although this may sound like pedantic advice to Latin American theologians by a European theologian.

The Spanish word *pueblo* means 'people', but it also has at least two special shades of meaning which are not in themselves to be found in other living languages. *El pueblo* is the people (a) in the formal sense as a collective reality that is a factor acting in history and (b) the term also refers formally and in the concrete local situation to the majority of the people, in other words, to the poor in that locality or country. Used in this second sense, it has something in common with one of the meanings of the biblical concept *anawim*, 'the poor of the country'. The term *el pueblo* therefore has biblical credentials and 'the poor' are those people who have no voice or rather who have a voice, but a one which is not heard and which others often do not want to hear, because what it expresses for them is an accusation, the 'complaint of the people' rising up to heaven, and it is a voice that is heard by God, a God who sooner or later will call on a new Moses to set his people free.

The 'people's Church', then, is a Church of the poor masses, a Church that looks after the poor and at the same time is the collectivity of the poor, who are, as the poor, the 'subject of being the Church', compressed together in an '*oikoumene* of suffering ones' gathered around the Lord. There is certainly a 'performative' element in this Latin American way of speaking about the 'people's Church', implying that the official Church is not (although it ought to be) a 'Church of the poor' and that it is often not on their side, but on the side of the powerful and therefore (although this is not the intention) in fact against the poor. The official Church is therefore also partisan. There is also an echo of already fulfilled hope in the term 'people's Church', a suggestion that manifestations of the 'Church of the poor' are already clearly present here and there, manifestations that are increasing in number and can no longer be checked. This Church of the poor already has its own martyrs and martyrdom has since time immemorial been the 'seed' of Christian faith.

In so far as I have been able to ascertain, Bishop Romero never used the term *iglesia popular* in his sermons and writings. He probably deliberately avoided the term in order not to give rise to misunderstandings. All the same, he was very concerned to express the conviction that the Church, as inspired by the Gospel, should take root and find its focal point in the poor, to whom the Gospel was, in an Isaian manner, proclaimed and who were themselves becoming proclaimers of the Gospel—subjects of being the Church and of the Church's priestly, pastoral and prophetic ministry. What we have here, then, is the formation in a socio-historical context of a Church community that is in no way alien to the spirit of the New Testament. It cannot be disputed, of course, that a certain separation has come about in this situation, not in itself between the people and the bishops (as has been suggested in certain quarters), but certainly between the poor and the rich. But then Paul himself criticised not the poor, but the rich in a similar situation, when he asked: 'Do you despise the Church of God and humiliate those who have nothing? What shall I say to you? Shall I commend you in this? No, I will not!' (1 Cor. 11:22).

The Church's new Code of Canon Law repeats the very fortunate statement of Vatican II, speaking of the local churches, of which the one Catholic Church consists (can. 368) and saying that the 'one, holy Catholic and apostolic Church of Christ' is really present and active in the local churches (can.369). The universal Church, then, is also present and living in a Church of the poor. The official ministries have therefore to be carried out in the concrete in these local churches within a clear context and in the light of the great Christian tradition. It is simply not possible for theologians or sociologists to ascertain by study and reflection the concrete form that the offices in a Church of the poor will take. This can only be done in a permanent process of theological reflection about what is in fact taking place in the building up of communities in the already existing local churches. Inspired by the Gospel, leaders arise naturally, take initiatives and fulfil what is known in the Christian tradition as the ecclesial meaning of 'office'.

The only question that remains to be answered is: Should there or should there not be ordination? The southern countries differ from the northern ones here. In northern Europe, we are concerned with a pure theology of office, but theologians in the countries of the South tend to solve this problem pragmatically and are only concerned that what is necessary for the evangelical vitality of Christian communities should take place. In my opinion, both points of view go back to similar although divergent theological concerns. The pragmatic theologians believe that the existing threefold division of the Church's office (episcopate, presbyterate and diaconate) can be left as it is (in view of the attitude of those in authority in the Church) and they are therefore not really interested in any sacramental 'merging' or *ordinatio*. In my opinion, it would be ecclesiologically wrong to do what has sometimes been done in Europe, namely to identify 'ordination' with clericalisation and on the basis of this identification encourage an attitude of awe in the presence of every ordination.

The theoreticians' attitude towards this pragmatic view is that the threefold division of office that has existed since time immemorial does not in any sense stand in the way of new forms of office that may eventually emerge. No one will of course object to the phenomenon of as many Christians as possible committing themselves to the building up of the Church—that is, after all, the task of all Christians. It is also not a phenomenon that will do away with the specific sacramental aspect of office in the Church. I am personally therefore in favour of a suitable form of ordination (a laying on of hands accompanied by a special *epiclesis* that is specific to office) for those who have in recent years emerged as 'animators' of these ecclesial communities of the poor.

Translated by David Smith

Notes

1. Y. Congar *Jalons pour une théologie du laicat* (Paris 1953; 2nd edn. with addenda 1964).
2. Stephen of Tournai (d. 1203) *Summa*, Prologue.
3. *Decretalia* VII, 12, q. 1; ed. Friedberg I, 678.
4. A. Faive *Naissance d'une hierarchie. Les premières étapes du cursus clérical* (Paris 1977).
5. G. Dautzenberg 'Zur Stellung der Frauen in den paulinischen Gemeinden' *Die Frau im Urchristentum* (Freiburg 1983) pp. 182–224 and especially pp. 214–221; E. Schüssler-Fiorenza In Memory of Her. *A Feminist Theological Reconstruction of Christian Origins* (New York 1983) pp. 205–218.
6. Ambrosiaster *Ad Ephesios* 4, 12. 1–4 (CSEL Ambrosiaster III, 81, 99).
7. See especially P. J. Cordes *Sendung zum Dienst: Exegetisch-systematische Studien zum Konzilsdebat 'Vom Dienst und Leben der Priester'* (Frankfurt 1972) especially pp. 202 and 291–301.
8. Quoted by P. Pourrat *Le Sacerdoce: doctrine de l'Ecole Française* (Paris 1947) pp. 44ff.
9. J. H. Newman *Select Treatises of St Athanasius* (Oxford 2nd edn. 1888); H. E. Manning *The Eternal Priesthood* (London 20th edn. 1930).
10. See for a more complete analysis of this history my new book *Christelijke identiteit en ambten in de Kerk. Een pleidooi voor mensen in de Kerk* (Baarn 1984).

Virgil Elizondo
Leonardo Boff

EPILOGUE

Throughout this issue we have striven to bring out the many aspects of the new forms of Church life which are emerging as more and more of the masses of the poor find new life in their response of faith to the Word of the Lord. We have heard from the various continents and the reports are truly astounding and inspiring. Truly a new Pentacost is taking place. From being passive participants in the rituals of the Church, the people are being transformed into active Christians who seek to participate fully in the life and mission of the Church. As in the early days of the Church, great numbers are added to the ranks of dynamic church membership each day. This should surely be a great source of rejoicing for the entire Church.

As we worked on this issue and reviewed the various articles, it became evident that as good and as representative as the articles are, they did not do justice to the actual situation. It is much better and far more vast than the articles bring out. They expose but the tip of the iceberg of the contemporary phenomenon of the Spirit that is currently taking place in many Christian areas of the Third World. In sharp contrast to the European experience of the recent past when the masses of the working people were lost from the Church, it is precisely the masses of the poor and the working classes that are shouting with spontaneous joy and profound conviction: We are Church! The Church is alive and vibrant among these Christians.

As we read through the testimonies and recalled our own personal experiences, we were deeply impressed by the evidence of the envangelical power, the ecclesial awareness and the Christian spirituality which is evident throughout the articles. Yet, nothing new, no matter how good it might be, begins without opposition, suffering and pain—like the birth of a child.

Behind all this ecclesial activity, there is an underlying theology which needs to be explored, elaborated and announced. This theological reflection does not emanate out of the aulas of the universities but out of the common struggle of the theologians together with the believing community to reflect and articulate the meaning of their faith in a critical and ecclesial way.

The theological reflection which comes out of these new experiences of Church has always questioned all elements of the *status quo* which have functioned in favour of the powerful and against the powerless. Hence, it itself has always been questioned and attacked by those who have found comfort and security in the structures of the past. The elaboration of the theology which emerges out of the ecclesial experience of the poor has been increasingly under attack by society, lay groups, business groups, bishops and Roman Curia.

The attacks have not been confined to Church circles, even official reports to the US political and business community consider this type of theological reflection one of the greatest threats to the business interests of the United States. Today, the well-publicised Ratzinger report, which the cardinal himself claims to be a private and unofficial paper, is consistently being used against the theological efforts which emerge out of the poor.

In view of this, *Concilium* dedicated a portion of its annual meeting to the analysis of the situation in which this is taking place. It seems that all the struggles of the marginated for full inclusion in the Church (e.g. the women's questions and the cultural questions of the peoples of non-Western cultures) are running into increasing obstacles and difficulties. We lament the fact that it seems to us quite clear and self-evident that there are serious efforts on the part of many responsible people, even at the highest level of the Roman Curia, to discredit the insertion of the Church in the life and struggles of the poor. We cannot understand this fear. At the moment of history when the poor are finding new life and hope in their active and dynamic participation in the life of the Church and society, the very Church which has called them to life seems to be making every effort to discourage their new life. This is both painful and scandalous.

The very objective of the struggles of the basic Christian ecclesial communities, as is consistently brought out throughout this number, is to make the Kingdom of God and its promises evermore present among the poor. The theology which arises out of these Christian communities is characterised by a strong ecclesial insertion—the profound desire to be Church and to be a responsible part of the universal Church.

The situation of these new experiences is like that of a young child beginning to take its first steps. Yet the older folk, rather than showing excitement about its efforts to walk, seem to be making every effort to step upon the young child and crush it. But the efforts to destroy will not succeed. Its new life is not given to it by any human power but by the very God who is calling the people out of death into a new existence. These are painful beginnings, but they are joyful, full of the paschal joy which guarantees us that even if we are murdered we will not be destroyed because the God of life will protect us and bring us unto the fullness of life.

Biographical Note

GIUSEPPE ALBERIGO was born in Varese in 1926 and lectures at the Faculty of Political Studies at Bologna University. He is also Secretary of the Institute of Religious Studies in Bologna, editor of the quarterly Review *Cristianesimo nella Storia*, and a member of the international committee of *Concilium*. His publications include books on the Council of Trent, the development of the concept of power in the Church, Collegiality and Pope John XXIII, the genesis of *Lumen Gentium* and Conciliarism.

LEONARDO BOFF was born in Brazil in 1938 and teaches dogmatic and systematic theology at Petrópolis. He is editor of the *Revista eclesiástica Brasiliera* and of the Brazilian edition of *Concilium*. He is the author of several books, including *Jesus Christ Liberator* (1979), *The Maternal Face of God* (1980), *Life according to the Spirit* (1981), and a study of St Francis, *Do lugar do Pobre* (From the Place of the Poor) (1984).

ENRIQUE DUSSEL was born in 1934 in Mendoza, Argentine. He holds doctorates in philosophy from Madrid and in history from the Sorbonne, and in 1981 received an honorary doctorate in theology from the university of Fribourg. He is professor of the history of theology and of the history of the Latin American church at the Instituto Teologico de Estudios Superiores in Mexico, and president of the newly formed commission for the study of the history of the Latin American church (CEHILA). Among his recent writings are *History of the Church in Latin America (1492–1979)* (1981); *Praxis latinoamericana y filosofia de la liberacion* (1983); *Philosophy of Liberation* (forthcoming).

CASIANO FLORISTÁN was born in 1926 at Arguedas (Spain). He studied chemistry at Zaragoza, philosophy at Salamanca and theology at Innsbruck, and was ordained priest in 1956. He was awarded a doctorate in 1959 at Tübingen. Since 1960, he has been a teaching professor at the Pontifical University of Salamanca in the Department of Pastoral Studies in Madrid. He was Principal of the Higher Pastoral Institute of Madrid from 1963–1973. He is president of the John XXIII Association of Theologians of Spain. Since 1973, he has been giving courses in Pastoral Theology in the United States. His publications include: *La vertiente pastoral de la sociología religiosa* (1960), *La parroquia, comunidad eucarística* (1961), *El año litúrgico* (1962), *Teología de la acción pastoral* (1968), *El catecumenado* (1972), *La evangelización, tarea del cristiano* and is co-author of *Conceptos fundamentales de pastoral* (1983).

ALOIS LORSCHEIDER, OFM, was born in Southern Brazil in 1924. He joined the Franciscan Order and was ordained in 1948, taking a doctorate in theology at the Antonianum in Rome in 1952. Consecrated bishop in 1962, he moved as archbishop to Fortaleza in the North-East of Brazil in 1973, and was made a cardinal by Pope Paul VI in 1976. He has been president of the Brazilian Bishops' Conference and of CELAM. His published work consists mainly of articles on Vatican II, on Puebla (where he was co-president), and on theology for preaching and life.

CARLOS MANUEL SANCHEZ is a coordinator in a basic community in Managua, Nicaragua.

URIEL MOLINA OLIÚ, OFM, was born in 1932 in Matagalpa, Nicaragua. He joined the Order of Friars Minor, of the Province of Assisi, in 1953, and after completing his novitate studied theology in the Franciscan Seminary in Perugia. He was ordained priest in 1958. After further studies in Rome and Jerusalem, he was awarded the degree of Doctor of Theology. He returned to Nicaragua in 1965 and was appointed to the parish of Santa María de los Angeles in El Riguero, a deprived district of Managua. In 1966 he became Professor of Theology in the Central American University of the Jesuit Fathers in Managua. He was professor for five years, and has been a parish priest for nineteen years. In 1979 he founded the Antonio Valdivieso Ecumenical Centre in Managua, to offer support to Christians involved in revolution.

JOHN MUTISO-MBINDA is a priest of Machakos Diocese in Kenya. He studied sociology at Syracuse University and worked in a rural parish in his home diocese for three years before taking up a job as lecturer in African pastoral anthropology at the AMECEA Pastoral Institute (Gaba) for six years. Since 1982 he has been Secretary General of the Association of the Member Episcopal Conferences in Eastern Africa (AMECEA). His publications include 'Ecumenism as a Pastoral Priority' *AFER* 22, No. 3 (1980) 145–150; 'Inculturation and African Local Church' *Collection: African Theology*, Report of the Yaounde Meeting, September 24–28, 1980, Ecumenical Association of African Theologians, Yaounde, Cameroun, pp. 37–50 (also published under the title 'Inculturacion e Iglesia local Africana' in *Missiones Extranjeras* (Madrid 1982) Nos. 70–71, pp. 331–346); 'Progress Towards Unity: Sixth Assembly of WCC' *AFER* 25, No. 5 (1983) 266–274; 'The Eucharist and the Family—in an African Setting' *AMECEA Documentation Service* (Nairobi 1984), ADS 84/No. 282, 1–6; 'The Church and Human Rights in Africa' *IMCS Documentation and Information Centre* (Nairobi 1984), Doc. No. 1, pp. 1–6.

JORGE PIXLEY, the son of American Baptist missionaries, spent his first 18 years in Managua, Nicaragua, where he did his elementary and secondary studies. He studied theology and biblical studies at the University of Chicago. For twenty years he has been Professor of Bible in three schools, the Evangelical Seminary of Puerto Rico, the Lutherian Faculty of Theology (Argentine), and the Baptist Seminary of Mexico. Among his books are *Reino de Dios* (1977), translated into English as *God's Kingdom* (1981), *El libro de Job: Comentario bíblico latinoamericano* (1982), and *Exodo: una lectura evangélica y popular* (1983).

PEDRO RIBEIRO DE OLIVEIRA was born in Minas Gerais, Brazil, in 1943. He received his doctorate in sociology from the Catholic University of Louvain, and lectures in sociology at the Pontifical University of Rio de Janeiro. He has published several articles in the *Rev. Ecles. Bras.*, mainly on popular Catholicism and the Basic Communities, and has collaborated in books on authority and participation (1973) and Catholic Charismatic Renewal (1977).

PABLO RICHARD was born in 1939 in Chile. He gained a licentiate in theology from the Catholic University of Chile, a licentiate in scripture from the Pontifical Biblical Institute in Rome, a doctorate in sociology from the Sorbonne and a doctorate *honoris causa* from the Free Faculty of Protestant Theology in Paris. At present, he is professor of theology at the National University of Costa Rica and a member of the Ecumenical Research Department in Costa Rica and of the Commission for Church History Studies of South America. His publications include *Christianismo, lucha ideológica y racionalidad socialista* (1975), *Cristianos por el socialismo* (1976), *La Iglesia latino-americana entre el temor y la esperanza* (1980), *Morte das cristandades e nascimento da Igreja* (1982); he was editor of

Materiales para una historia de la teología en América Latina (1981) and co-editor of *La Iglesia de los Pobres en América Central* (1982).

EDWARD SCHILLEBEECKX, OP, was born at Antwerp (Belgium) in 1914 and was ordained in 1941. He studied at Louvain, Le Saulchoir, the Ecole des Hautes Etudes and the Sorbonne (Paris). He became a doctor of theology in 1951 and magister in 1959. Since 1958, he has been teaching dogmatic theology and hermeneutics at the University of Nijmegen (the Netherlands). He is the editor-in-chief of the Dutch theological review *Tijdschrift voor Theologie*. His works in English translation include the following: *Christ, the Sacrament of the Encounter with God* (1963); *The Understanding of Faith* (1974); *Jesus. An Experiment in Christology* (1979); *Christ. The Experience of Jesus as Lord* (New York 1980) (= *Christ. The Christian Experience in the modern World* London 1980); *Jesus and Christ. Interim Report on the Books Jesus and Christ* (1980); *Ministry. Leadership in the Community of Jesus Christ* (New York 1981) (= *Ministry. A Case for Change* London 1981).

LEONOR TELLERÍA is a coordinator in a basic community in the Ducali district of Managua in Nicaragua.

CARLOS ZARCO MERA is animator in a basic ecclesial community in Mexico City.

CONCILIUM 1983

NEW RELIGIOUS MOVEMENTS

Edited by John Coleman and Gregory Baum   161

LITURGY: A CREATIVE TRADITION

Edited by Mary Collins and David Power   162

MARTYRDOM TODAY

Edited by Johannes-Baptist Metz and
Edward Schillebeeckx   163

CHURCH AND PEACE

Edited by Virgil Elizondo and Norbert Greinacher   164

INDIFFERENCE TO RELIGION

Edited by Claude Geffré and Jean-Pierre Jossua   165

THEOLOGY AND COSMOLOGY

Edited by David Tracy and Nicholas Lash   166

THE ECUMENICAL COUNCIL AND THE CHURCH CONSTITUTION

Edited by Peter Huizing and Knut Walf   167

MARY IN THE CHURCHES

Edited by Hans Küng and Jürgen Moltmann   168

JOB AND THE SILENCE OF GOD

Edited by Christian Duquoc and Casiano Floristán   169

TWENTY YEARS OF CONCILIUM— RETROSPECT AND PROSPECT

Edited by Edward Schillebeeckx, Paul Brand and
Anton Weiler   170

All back issues are still in print: available from bookshops (price £3.50) or direct
from the publisher (£3.85/US$7.45/Can$8.55 including postage and packing).

T. & T. CLARK LTD, 36 GEORGE STREET, EDINBURGH EH2 2LQ, SCOTLAND

X